Small Acts of Disappearance

Small Acts of

Fiona Wright

GIRA —
MOND

Disappearance

Essays on Hunger

First published in 2015
from the Writing & Society Research Centre
at the University of Western Sydney
by the Giramondo Publishing Company
PO Box 752
Artarmon NSW 1570 Australia
www.giramondopublishing.com

Designed by Harry Williamson
Typeset by Andrew Davies
in 11.25/14 pt Garamond 3

Printed and bound by Ligare Book Printers
Distributed in Australia by NewSouth Books

National Library of Australia
Cataloguing-in-Publication data:

Wright, Fiona
Small acts of disappearance: essays in hunger

ISBN 978-1-922146-93-9 (pbk)

362.25092

9 8 7 6 5 4 3 2 1

For my sisters: by blood, in-law and in arms

I speak of those years when I lived
walled alive in myself, left with nothing
but the inward search for joy, for a word
that would ruffle the plumage of mind
to reach its tenderest down;
when consuming myself I endured,
but could not change.

GWEN HARWOOD 'Past and Present'

Contents

IN COLOMBO

I'll always remember the particular intensity that malnutrition brings on, I know that I miss it still. That alertness of sensation, where every minute cell in the body is awake and alive to the smallest details of the outside world. I've been told this is instinctual, a biological reaction to the threat that the hungry body perceives itself to be under; that a malnourished animal is weaker, more vulnerable to predators, and compensates by trying to pick up on danger early enough to still be able to escape. The world glistens in this state of apprehension. Your skin prickles. When I was travelling in this state, so many days felt strangely brittle, saturated, super-real.

Even now, I find it hard to separate what I experienced in Sri Lanka from what I experienced in my body, to figure out how much of my perception was sharpened by my hunger, how much by the complicated novelty and otherness that travel always involves. At that stage, it was three years since I had fallen ill, but only eighteen months since the very rare and still-untreatable cause of my persistent vomiting had been identified. But I'm not sure if the ground hadn't already shifted again then, if the physical disease hadn't taken on the disordered dimensions that I'm fighting to this day.

I've also discovered, since my diagnosis, that even specialist opinion has shifted as to the nature of that physical condition. Rumination is a muscular tic of the upper stomach and its sphincter. Like any muscular tic it is unconscious and uncontrollable, but at least in part psychosomatic. This doesn't make it any less bodily, any less real. When I was finally diagnosed, the first thing the specialist said was 'You're not making this up and you're not going mad'; and eight years later the condition was added to the *Diagnostic and Statistical Manual of Mental Disorders*, the DSM, which is the standard classification manual for mental health used by psychiatrists worldwide.

I travelled to Sri Lanka three years before I stepped for the first time inside the office of a psychologist, five years before I fully realised that there was more to my illness, to my hunger, than simple physicality. But I sometimes think that it was here, in Colombo, that things changed, and my illness grew more complicated. Even so, I never can tell to what degree pathology stood between me and the country that I came to love, or if I ever could have done things differently.

On my first day in Colombo, I wrote in my journal that the light seemed golden, that I'd felt pure joy on seeing so many animals – monkeys and lizards, crows and cows – wandering the red-earthed streets. On my second day, unable to properly pronounce the name of the suburb in which I was living, I got completely lost, riding in the backseat of a three-wheeler taxi, until the driver tried to kiss me in an unmapped alley. I ended up walking in the late-season rain, along streets that had no footpaths, to the low-roofed house where I was billeted to a Sinhalese family, then standing, silent and shaking, at my bedroom window, which overlooked a primary school, the children in immaculate white uniforms running on the pressed dirt of its playground. I already felt too small for the situation I'd placed myself in, alone and as-yet untravelled, in a part of the world I knew almost nothing about.

On my third day in Colombo, I started work. I arrived early at the offices of the local English-language newspaper where I was interned, and my section editor immediately assigned me to a story on the street children of the city. I'm still not sure if she was deliberately trying to provoke me, fresh off the plane as I was, to throw my complacent, sunburnt skin into a world that I had little comprehension of. Anesha, a young and quiet colleague with a thick wave of hair reaching right to her waist, accompanied me to translate. We took a driver, and a van, my digital camera. I'd had half a piece of strangely sweet toast with imported Marmite for breakfast. My billet family had bought the Marmite for me from a small grocer near their house; it was stocked alongside Diet Coke, pasta, and toilet paper on a shelf labelled 'Western Items' near the back of the store.

I never found out the names of the places we went to that day, I never went through them again in my whole time in the city. We drove to a rubbish tip beside a timber train station, untouched since the so-called *British era*, the thick awnings corroded with insect bole, a round rust-coloured clock unmoving above the entrance, looking for signs of hungry children. Shredded pieces of black plastic flapped at our approach, and fat crows stared us down, but otherwise there was stillness, just hot silence. At high noon, we reached a string of *kovils*, the intricately sculpted, intensely-coloured Hindu temples worshipped in by what remains of Colombo's Tamil population.

These too were built beside a garbage ground, dotted with small timber stalls where women sold strings of marigolds and enormous platters of tropical fruit, to leave as offerings inside the shadowed temples. Anesha pointed out the separate kovil for the women, the ripe-looking goddesses dancing along the length of each steeple, the pawpaws cut open and rotting by the door, in petition for fertility. She bought one for me. I was twenty-three, and had no babies. I also hadn't bled for three whole years. Inside, I watched a series of young women bash coconuts against their heads, then bow before a painted goddess in an alcove.

Outside, Anesha was waiting, squatting on her heels beside a woman with a small child in her lap. The child wore a faded polo-shirt, no pants, and put his fingers to his mouth as I approached. What did I want to ask? Anesha said. The sun was beating on my back, a small, black fly crawling on my forearm, the red leather of my shoes constricting in the heat. The child kept gesturing his fingers to his mouth. His mother said that he was five years old, and wouldn't allow him to be photographed in case his school teachers and classmates found out that he was homeless.

At the other end of town, Anesha and the driver stopped for juice and cutlets, little fried fish croquettes wrapped in old school worksheets which soaked up the oil into transparent patches. I bought a bottle of water, alert and strong.

We spoke to a girl that day who lived beneath tarpaulins on the outskirts of De Soysa Circus, a sweeping boulevard near the centre of the city, which once went by the name of Lipton Circus. She was pretending to play cricket with her brothers as we approached, miming the actions of bowling and batting at a non-existent ball. She was beautiful. The skin on her shins was thick and grey and shiny. She told me that she liked to watch the women going to Odel, Colombo's large department store, just across the road, and to pretend that she was going shopping too.

I never figured out how to cope with waste in a place like Colombo, in a country where so many have so little so much of the time, where the amount I could earn in one day of resented office work would house a family for a week. How to understand hunger when it leapt so suddenly from something abstract in the wider world, and a state suppressed within myself, to something many-faced, insistent and ever-present. Where the food that I threw out could get this child, in her undersized dress, out from underneath her tarpaulin and to school. In my first days back home, in suburban Sydney, I stood paralysed in the vegetable aisle of the supermarket, unable to choose between the six different varieties of onion. I bought cherries, in mid-winter. I didn't eat them.

Hunger is only political, only poignant when it is abnormal, when it is unusual and strange: in a place were hunger is so prevalent, one hungry child with an imaginary cricket bat was just a colour piece in the weekend section of a newspaper. But my hunger, singular and self-circling, was a crisis in my hometown. It marked me out. I was wasteful, and I was distasteful. A car with wound-down windows once shot past me on the street, someone shouting from the backseat: 'Eat a hamburger, you bitch!'

My newspaper's office, such as it was, was just off the main street of the busy suburb of Borella, the site of the 1983 riots that are generally considered the start of Sri Lanka's civil war, a war which didn't end until 2009, three years after my first visit to the country. Here, in Borella, Tamil civilians were pulled from buses and killed; here, houses and cars were burned with whole families still inside. I was born in 1983. My colleagues, my age and younger, had never lived in anything other than that war, knew peace only as an abstract and alien thing. They hardly saw the soldiers on the street corner, leaning and leering against their rifles, the razor wire hung with drying washing, the concrete bollards. They lived in a city grown stagnant, its infrastructure unchanged because of the protracted military campaigns and clampdowns. There was a fervour the day I first brought my laptop in to work, so small and sleek beside the ancient office PCs. A doll-sized computer, my colleagues said, for a doll-sized human being. My newspaper, without a trace of irony, was called *The Nation*.

In the damp-walled *Nation* offices, we were given cups of tea each morning and early afternoon by one of the two tea-wallahs, employed purely for this purpose. It took three weeks before I learnt exactly how to ask for mine without the obligatory milk, the sugar thick enough to stand a spoon in: plain tea. 'Just leaves and water, miss?' the younger one would ask, wrinkling his high forehead in consternation. At lunchtime, one of the copy boys would often whip out his guitar and play old pop songs, barefoot, while others beat tricky percussion riffs on the edges of tables with their hands.

I was using the country, and *The Nation*, to cut my teeth. I know now that it's a fairly common practice for young and ambitious media graduates to take a placement at any one of the English-language newspapers that operate across the developing world, catering mostly to ex-pats, business people and the local Westernised elite. To come back with experience, a competitive advantage in what was, even then, a tricky industry to get a foot into. I wrote articles about animal charities, about fashion shows, about dog grooming, and about Sri Lanka's first writers' festival, held in Galle, the southernmost city of the island, which had been badly affected by the recent tsunami. In the evenings, I went to beachside bars or Colombo's only café with other journalists, film-makers, investment bankers, all of whom had been to university overseas, and very few of whom spoke either of Sri Lanka's native languages.

It's awful and it's dubious, of course, to use an entire country as a test ground, in a kind of personal experiment. It's the same unthinking privilege that any kind of travel is predicated on for we children of the West. But I also wanted to try to be someone else for a time – to be forcibly removed from the people who knew me, from my habits, from my patterns of behaviour, my routines and rules. I thought, perhaps, that distance could defeat disease, that I could leave my home and somehow leave my self behind as well.

Most of the journalists bought rice-and-curry lunch packets from a tiny kitchen down the road; wrapped into a neat newspaper mound, there'd be a tightly packed, square prism of white rice, a daub of different curries in each corner, coconut and chilli sambal in the middle. We mixed it all together with our fingers, the turmeric staining mine nicotine-yellow. The varieties of curry changed each day, dependent on what had been harvested: to not be able to choose was as terrifying as it was liberating.

The problem for me, in Sri Lanka, was that the country's cuisine is based on two ingredients that almost always triggered my vomiting – rice and the coconut milk that binds the sauce in any curry. The first time I ate one of these lunch packets with my colleagues, I had to sprint from the tea room to the small garden at the side of the office building. I threw up onto a bed of brightly-coloured tropical flowers and tried to shake off my workmates' well-meaning concern and questions. But I know too that I told the mother of my billeted family that I was a vegetarian, my new café-set friends that I couldn't eat gluten (and we all laughed that this was a Westerner's disease) – that I was limiting my options, even then, far beyond just what I knew my stomach couldn't handle.

I'd often wander further down beyond the kitchen instead, and buy a fist-sized egg roll, a soft bun slit down the middle and filled with slices of boiled egg and bright red sauce, as well as a tomato from a street stall. It cost me the equivalent of twenty cents. I started buying two each day, and handing one to the first beggar I encountered at the bus stop near the office. One of the beggars had some kind of fluid swelling in his feet, his ankles as round and wide as tree trunks. Another had a goitre that forced her head to crick permanently sideways on her neck, like a perpetually shrugged shoulder. At first, I'd eat the other roll, painfully slowly; I remember one colleague asking me, perplexed, if that was all a typical Westerner would eat for lunch. Eventually, I started working through the lunch break, a habit that I stuck to in the worst years of my illness for the way that this working pattern looks diligent and industrious, rather than insane.

There was a pharmacy too on the other side of the street, in the most modern and starkly tidy building in the area. It was the place my colleagues trooped to for the 'Nescafé machine', a contraption that squeezed wet and weak instant coffee out of little plastic sachets, or for packets of prawn crackers or tiny, salt-dried fish. It was here one afternoon that I was grabbed at by a woman in a sky-blue linen suit, her fingers pressing into the thin flesh of my upper arms. 'I can see you, sad little lady,' she whispered in my ear. She stared at me, unashamedly, she asked me immediately about my faith, about my marriage, both of which are non-existent. The woman grasped my arm and held my hand against her chest. 'I think that God has put me in your life today for a reason. To bless you. To make you well.' I tried to move away; but she followed me, unable as I was to blend into the background, the whole way back into the office, where the tea-wallah hustled her away.

Each day I caught two buses into work, juddering and lumbering things, occasionally riddled with holes in the floor that were plastered over with gaffer tape or cardboard. They were crowded of a morning, fuggy and sticky in the afternoon, and always full, and the crush was perfect for hiding the wandering hands of commuting men. At first, I thought the frequent brushes against my body were accidental, and very often, they were carefully construed to leave plenty of room for doubt. One man might look like he was nodding off, his hand relaxed and floppy against the backrest of the seat, until it slowly started rubbing at my breasts. Another might hold a satchel at waist-height and then repeatedly bump against my thighs. My knees grew bruises.

Each day, I changed buses at Nugegoda Junction, where a white plaster Buddha sat smiling at the smog beneath the heart-shaped leaves of a spindly Bodhi tree. The ground was clayey and red there. Three weeks after I returned to Australia, a bomb was detonated in the dress shop on the corner.

The Sri Lankan wolf-whistle is a kind of sucking noise, fish-like through pursed lips. It took me some time to understand this, the strange sound that pursued me through the street. I'd not known before what it means to be so conspicuous, to be recognised and remembered. At a time when I was slowly being pared back to my bones, when I was every day becoming insubstantial, I've never felt so looked-at, so fully bodied.

What disturbed me most about this was how quickly I became accustomed to being looked at, even touched. My body, in public, was public. I lowered my gaze to the ground.

The women in my office nodded along when I complained. It happened to them too — most of them found other ways to come to work, or always travelled with their families. Shezny, a wide-smiled Tamil woman, said that when she had to catch a bus alone, she'd wear an extra pin inside her sari, to jab at anyone who touched her up. 'That's great,' I laughed, 'you take a little prick all of your own!'

'No, no,' she said, bewildered. 'A sari pin is very large.'

I never saw other women walking on the streets, save for an occasional pair of white-robed nuns, holding hands and turning inward. I rarely saw other women in public at all; there was no space for their bodies in the civil life of this city. My female colleagues were unusual because they were employed, all the more so because they worked in offices instead of hospitals or schools – but even they all spoke to me about how much they wanted to get married, to find a husband, to find love. Weeks in, I realised that they were daughters until the day they became wives; they were women before they were people. They could never move beyond their bodies, never forget that their bodies were there. But here was I, living beside them in a body that was slowly disappearing, despite its new conspicuousness. They took me into their houses, taught me to cook traditional meals that take hours to prepare, and I pushed the food around on my plate, unsure whether it was more polite to not eat the meal they had served me at all, or to eat it and then throw up immediately afterwards.

My collarbones grew angular enough to become individually sunburnt.

When I left Sri Lanka, at the end of my internship and far too sick to stay, I was light-headed and felt almost absent as I walked the streets, as if everything inside my skull had been untethered. I felt that time itself had swollen in the pre-monsoon humidity and was moving in thick and syrupy globs. I was wearing a child's salwar kameez, the long shirt and baggy pants worn by the country's Muslim women, the fabric barely stretched across my shrunken breasts. I'd chosen the salwar because it was a chaste woman's clothing, the throat, the knees, the shoulders covered by brightly-coloured cloth; I had found that it deterred, at least a little, the groping hands on buses. In my first days back in Sydney, I was shocked when I saw a young woman in hotpants. The speed at which my body had taken Colombo underneath its skin surprised me. Smaller, slower-paced, and thicker-tongued, I no longer fitted neatly in the space I'd left behind.

I became obsessed with automation, with the small mechanised tasks that in Colombo had all been performed by quiet men in meticulous uniforms, that had been physical and bodied, but now were strangely abstract. Within a week I was back in my old job, driving in along the M5 through toll-gates that opened automatically in response to the infra-red tag on my front windscreen, swiping a card to open the office building's doors, swiping again to activate a lift. My computer automatically opened the schedule of radio programs I was to monitor each day.

There was a modicum of safety, somehow, in the constant small human interactions that were still in place in Colombo's public spaces. Here, I thought, it would be easy just to disappear.

For a long time, I couldn't place exactly what it was, the thing that took so long for me to reconcile. I came home feeling different, looking diminished, and unable to tie together the two cities I now loved, and the very different ways of being that each engendered. I think now that what I struggled with was my own dreadful inconsistency, what it means to love a place and a people in the way I did Colombo, and yet to have held it at such distance, however unwittingly. In many ways, my hunger kept me separate, unable to participate fully in those myriad rituals of society and sociability that circle around food, unable to accept nourishment from the same places as the people I was living with, or from the very people I was moving amongst. Hunger forces a kind of refusal, a brutal, impenetrable independence, leaves us quite literally unable to break bread and connect with the people in our orbit; I realise now that this is how I've lived most of my adult life.

But more than this, in Colombo, my hunger was obscene. It was not predicated on need, on poverty or parentlessness or war, corruption or greed. It was something feeding on and off itself, something always leading back into itself – the starving brain turned inwards to survive. My hunger was not, and could not, be equated with the hunger that I saw around me. Amongst so much need, my own denial was something as incomprehensible to my local friends as the hunger they lived alongside was to me. Something irreconcilable here made my world grow bigger and more disparate, and all the while, I shrank. And I shrank away as well.

IN HOSPITAL

At my sickest, a lover once folded a blanket over my shoulderblade before curling against my back to sleep. People visibly recoiled when I passed, or looked back over their shoulders in a double take that I could never help but notice. From the outside, nobody understands the seemingly wilful hunger of those of us who waste away, nobody really understands the hold that it can have, its awful power.

I know now that the impulse I have to starve comes from exactly the same place as my impulse to write: hunger, like writing, is a mediator. It stands between me and the world, between my self and the things that might cause it harm. Hunger is addictive, and it is intensely sensual, pulling the body between extremes of hyper-alertness and a foggy trance-like dream state. And like writing, it lets me stand clear, separate and intact; it lets me stand on the outside.

I spent years determined to stay on the outside. Because I wasn't, I was sure, one of *those women*.

The problem, I realise now, was that I'd never met one of those women. I never really did until my first admission to a hospital day program, five years after my travel to Sri Lanka.

When I agreed to the admission, I still didn't think that I belonged in an eating disorder program, that my hunger was malicious. I knew that I was noticeably underweight, and that I was still struggling to manage my physical condition, to eat enough to fuel my body without throwing up in the process. I'd scan every restaurant that I went to upon entering, to make sure that I was seated close to the bathroom or the door; I had become adept on picnics and at parties, ducking out, mid-conversation, and scampering for the nearest plant or wheelie bin. ('Fucking junkie' a man once spat as he walked past me, when I was doubled over behind a tree after an early café breakfast with my best friend.)

By the time I was admitted, I'd spent two years visiting an outpatient clinic, at first fortnightly, then monthly, walking past the locked psychiatric ward and up three flights of stairs to its set of narrow corridors; at the height of my illness, even this exertion left me dizzy and unsteady on my feet. I still thought that my main problem was anxiety, that the stress and exhausting worry that were constantly coursing through me were exacerbating the vomiting that was the main symptom of my physical illness. I never once thought that the way that I was eating might be exacerbating the stress with which my body and my mind were both racked. A psychologist had slowly encouraged me to attend the clinic, suggesting only, carefully, that the doctors there would be experts at putting broken, undernourished bodies like my own back together. I remember showing the clinic's dietician, during my first appointment, the food diaries I'd been asked to keep over the preceding fortnight, and stating straight up, 'I'm not anorexic.' I didn't realise then that she must hear this all the time, and barely registered her response, 'You certainly eat as if you are.'

In these two years, I hardly progressed at all. I realise now this was mostly because I could not recognise the complex nature of my hunger, and so I couldn't understand the help the doctors there were trying to extend to me. I went alone to these appointments, waiting on one of the plastic armchairs lined up in a row past the reception desk, always alongside other thin and anxious women with flaking skin and darting eyes and knees that were constantly jigging up and down, out of both nervousness and a desire to burn more energy. I didn't talk to them, tried to avoid their gaze.

I can't remember, now, what I talked about with the psychiatrist in my appointments, my memories of these visits are cloudy with a strange combination of malnutrition, boredom, exhaustion and fear. But I do remember the one day that my regular doctor was away; his substitute was forthright, crisp and far less gentle in her manner than he had ever been. She said, after closing my by now bulky file,

'You know you're not getting anywhere here,' and I had to concede that she was right.

I called the hospital from a café up the road from the clinic, feeling somehow, and somewhat irrationally, that the decision to do so wasn't really mine to make, that my hand had finally been forced. I'm also not sure that I would ever have gone ahead with the admission if I hadn't thought that I would write about it later. But even as I walked, on the first day of my admission, through the building's bright blue door, after a round of meetings, measures, blood tests, heart checks and the reading of a rule book as thick as my spindly wrist, I still remember thinking, even then, that I'd have nothing in common at all with any of the other women I might meet there.

Because I wasn't, I thought, one of these women.

One woman hadn't had a bath in seven years, and always showered in the dark. Another would spend eight-hundred dollars every week on groceries, and seven hours vomiting each night, the blood vessels beneath her eyes bursting with the pressure. One had permanent callouses above the knuckles on her right hand, where they crashed against the backsides of her teeth. One woman walked circuits of a shopping centre so as to not be caught exercising, another had to wear padding underneath her feet in order to be able to walk at all. One woman stepped every hour, on the hour, onto her bathroom scales, another chewed eighteen packets of sugar-free gum each day. One would eat undercooked chicken once a month in the hope that she'd get salmonella. One would eat brussels sprouts for breakfast.

In the hospital, I bore these women a strange kind of witness; a split kind of witness, for weeks. Where I didn't want to be involved, didn't think myself included, but couldn't help but recognise myself reflected in the stories that they told. We moved our bodies in similar ways, curling our feet under the knobbled bases of our pelvises, bouncing our knees beneath the dining table as our meals were served, biting at our cuticles and lips. So too, the similarities between our secrets, the strange behaviour we tried to keep hidden, the discomfort we felt within our skins, were almost physical. I felt outside myself, borderless, I didn't know where witnessing stopped, and I began.

I kept a notebook in my first days in the hospital, but barely touched it. As I listened to the other women talk, hesitantly, at times angrily, often in tears, and I heard them voice so many of the things that I'd kept so long silent in myself, I knew immediately that it could never be my place to write about them, to speak for them, to use their stories to add colour to my own. I realised that these women were some of the bravest but also most vulnerable that I had ever met, and that to turn them into kooky characters in my writing would not only violate the privacy that the hospital was so careful to protect for us, but also do them violence. I realised, at last, that this story was not about them, but about me – even as I'd been denying that fact for years.

Under the hospital's supervised schedule of meals, I was suddenly forced to be without my hunger, and I walked out of the building every afternoon feeling skinless, almost painfully permeable. I walked down Broadway, the shuddering of trucks and passing buses vibrating through my bones, the footpath crumbly and frayed. I sometimes caught my reflection in the dark shop windows and was shocked by the glassiness of my own face. I'd buy a cold drink at the Hot Devil Bakery, defiantly sugarfree and fizzy. I'd sit quietly on the bus – I'd been forbidden to walk home, in case even this small act of exercise was a compulsion – and press my fingers against the stiff fibres of the seat, the cracked rubber seal of the window. These grubby, communal surfaces were a kind of landing pad. I couldn't change frequency so easily.

Because inside the hospital we were contained. Inside, no one could find what we said unimaginable. No one could think us stupid or indulgent or precious. No one was horrified when we cried over our plates of ravioli, limpid and almost visceral in its red sauce.

Our days, at least, had in-built structure. We arrived in time for morning tea and left forty-five minutes after afternoon tea, with lunch at 12:30 sharp. We were carefully watched during our meals: no breaking food up into little pieces, no eating food in any set order, no dunking biscuits in tea, no over-use of condiments, no counting chews, no reading labels, no tiny bites, no one thing left on the plate at all. Our meals were time-limited, with warnings given when we had ten, and then five minutes to go. One woman ate so slowly and tearfully that she had to shovel in most of her meal in overloaded forkfuls in those last minutes. Another tried to hide a whole potato in her pocket. We all hugged our stomachs and were silent after every meal. There was a grey box of tissues in the corner of the room.

We were weighed once a week, wearing pale-yellow paper gowns with elasticised cuffs and open backs, facing away from the numbers on the scale. We kept our gowns in a metal locker with ventilation gills, in zip-lock bags designed for storing food, our names written in texta on the label on the front: *Contents: Fiona.* Each afternoon, we picked up breakfast cereal, canned fruit and longlife milk in a brown paper bag to have for breakfast before we left home the next day. I turned the cereal into cookies and the tinned pears into cinnamon muffins and fed them to my family and friends. I didn't want to eat them, and couldn't bear to waste them, but the people I would give them to, I knew, would never think them a burden.

Every week, once a week, we were escorted outside, to practise eating in the world, where we knew our meals would not be correctly measured by a dietitian, where we'd have to choose, and where we could not be contained. Our first excursion was to a café on Glebe Point Road, we walked in the hot and stagey light of mid-afternoon, unspeaking, and in a ragged single file. I bit my lip, and felt it, full and sweet between my teeth. A dalmatian on a leash was curled in the doorway, it sniffed at the air as we entered and I was sure the café staff could smell fear on us too. We were given one minute each to place an order for a piece of cake. No one ordered coffee because we weren't allowed skim milk.

We were the biggest group in the café that day, and we'd walked beneath a building site to get there. A blond man in the scaffolding had wolf-whistled, at this group of young and slender women walking by.

Our days, at least, had in-built structure, to take advantage of the changes to our chronically starving brains, which had hardened, physiologically, into obsessionality and rigid, repeating patterns of thought and action. My hunger, and its rules, have been with me, always, for almost all of my adult life. My days have for so long been structured around meals, a constant accounting of what I have and haven't eaten, what I can and can't still eat, what I need to do to still feel safe. I still don't know who I am without my hunger; without its structures that support me too, its scaffolding.

Sometimes we went grocery shopping together, with an occupational therapist and a dietitan, and then cooked: we weighed out ingredients to the gram. We trimmed the smallest streaks of visible fat from our meat. One woman had no idea where to find butter in the supermarket aisles. Another refused to buy feta from the deli because it had no nutritional information panel. One had never before seen a leek. We wore blue latex gloves in the tiny kitchen, scrupulous about hygiene, and either tried to control each process as we cooked, or shrank back to avoid touching the ingredients entirely.

I had to leave the kitchen on the day we cooked risotto. I sat on the carpet in the next room, squeezing my temples with my knees. I already felt it choking up in my throat, as glutinous as craft glue.

This is the crux of it: what cannot be imagined from the outside, the breathless bodily panics, the unbrained terror, how I sweat and shake and bite down on my nails. I know it's inconceivable, outside, how the very idea of a plate of rice can make my mind seize up and stutter, as if the grains themselves were predatory. But this is how we lose our selves in this disease. We're instinctual in these moments, animal; and we're eaten up in each of these small acts of disappearance.

Inside the hospital building, a converted, two-storey house with high ceilings and a vague dampness in the walls, we waited a lot. We could listen to music, but not dance. We could stretch, but not walk around, we were forbidden to step into the small courtyard, lined with plane trees, at the back of the building. We weren't allowed to talk about what we'd eaten or why we were there, but it was impossible at times, not to mention the things that were obvious to us all. We stayed in the one room, its walls painted sky blue, its couches hard as lozenges, a whiteboard that was never really clean.

But what we found was solidarity, when none of us had felt solid, somehow, for years. Our exterior lives often had very little in common – in a discussion on exercise, for example, one woman added horse-riding and sailing to my suggestions of yoga or riding a bike. But our interior lives were as eerily congruent as project homes, though I'd spent at least eight years, by this stage, denying that we shared anything at all.

This was because my illness started with a physical condition, still very rare and very poorly understood. I was nineteen years old, and suddenly I was vomiting without any volition after most of my meals. It took almost eighteen months for my specialists to find a diagnosis, the weight dropping off a body that rapidly came to alarm me. I was advised to cut out of my diet the foods that I thought triggered the vomiting, and I did, by ever-increasing increments, until the ground shifted somewhere, and hunger became my safest state. Because my illness started with a physical condition, because I recognised, and didn't want and didn't like my too-thin body, because I didn't purge by conscious choice, because I was still eating, however limitedly, I thought that I was different. I realise now that this was partly because of my own misconceptions about the nature of anorexia, and the people who fall victim to it, but this is also the way the illness operates, by deception, by a long series of constraints that tighten so slowly that they're barely noticeable at all.

I thought, for so long, that I didn't have anything in common with these women, and I sometimes think that's the biggest tragedy of all. Because if I'd only recognised this earlier, before eight entire years of illness had gone by, I may have found the help I needed sooner. I may have been able to stave off my hunger before it managed to establish itself so fully and firmly in my life. I might, by now, be well.

One woman had slipped discs in her lower spine from vomiting, another had chronic bladder infections and damaged kidneys. One had had reconstructive surgery on her oesophagus because the juices of her stomach had been leaking into her lungs. Three women in their mid-twenties – myself included – had osteoporosis of the hips or spine.

One morning, about a month in, I realised that I'd been witness to the slow display of a quietly unfolding beauty in these women. That each week they grew more lovely. Some of this I'm sure was purely physical – the too-thin amongst us became less angular, our faces fuller, skin and hair alike lost their flakiness and pallor. So too our clothes looked better-tailored on our bodies. But it was more than this. I'd watched them all uncurl their tightened shoulders, unhang their heads, untuck their knees from underneath their chins. One woman, whose every word had seemed, at first, like it was being dragged out from her chest began to joke in a beautifully acerbic way, her mouth unpinched and her whole face softened around it; another had grown a laugh that shook the ceiling. This, I thought, is so much like a second adolescence, each time seeing a woman, glorious and gorgeous, emerge from somewhere underneath a brittle and anxious body. I went to a book launch one evening, and was told that I looked like a cherub with my newly-rounded cheeks.

I still knew that I would write about it later, and kept a vocab list on the back pages of my notebook. *You've been deskilled*, it says, *do some down-arrowing, take a helicopter view.* And *all of these rules you taught yourself.*

Shortly before my discharge I spent a Sunday in Thirroul, driving the hour-long coast road alone, a solitude I hadn't had for weeks. I was visiting three of my friends, all writers, who were staying in a barely-stable cottage on a cliff for the weekend. I felt relaxed on the road, I shouted along to songs with my windows wound down, and spent the afternoon sitting on the grass, watching the ocean. We took photos at lunch in a local café. The two boys went for a swim, and we two women talked about bodies, about illnesses, and about transition, about how hard it is to change. My friend hugged me when I left and I couldn't stop thinking, the whole way home, of the lamb sandwich sitting in my stomach, how we'd laughed at the waitress when she'd cleared the plates and said 'Too much bread is too much bread, you know?'

I didn't know how I could bring what we did inside the hospital out into the world. I didn't know if I'd be able to keep visible the things we'd given names to, the things we had made clear. *With symptom reduction comes space*, I had written in my notebook, but I didn't know if I could grow to fill the space I was discovering, if I'd be able to stay vigilant each day. I still don't know. I still, sometimes, am left bereft.

But what I hadn't expected was the heightened sensitivity when I came out. An instructor at my gym, a space I was protectively easing myself back into, equated the calories spent in one class with one small Easter bunny. 'You just worked off the ears!' she cried between songs, 'Now for the head!' A waiter brought a brownie to my table with my coffee and called me 'naughty'. I got angry when my mother tried to share her birthday chocolates, when my housemate had just honeyed toast for dinner, when a friend bought a dress that didn't fit because she was planning to lose weight after the holidays. When my university sent me an email about the Low-Fat Options Now Available on Campus.

I kept in contact with those women. About a month after the last of us was discharged, we met for a drink in a fairly new bar, just around the corner from the discreet, pebble-crete house where we had been confined. We all ordered vodka with lime and soda; fresh lime, not cordial, we all ignored the complimentary popcorn placed on a small tray before us. We sat on zebra-print couches, away from the door, where the first cold air of the season kept bursting through. One woman, the oldest among us, had worked for nearly ten years before her admission for Jenny Craig. She had needed to start fresh afterwards, and had found a job at a recruitment agency. She'd lost weight since I'd last seen her.

She had been to Friday drinks a few weeks into her new position, and after a few hours, a few beverages, one of her female colleagues had approached her at the bar. 'I'm onto you,' the colleague had said. 'You're a sister.'

'Sorry?' she stammered, 'A sister?'

'Were you AN or BN?' she asked.

She denied that she knew what her colleague meant, but was holding her wine glass before her, in that hand with the thick callouses raised above her knuckles – these are called Russell's Sign, after the doctor who first identified bulimia nervosa, BN, as a condition in its own right. The colleague laid her own knobbled fingers against them, and repeated:

'You're a sister.'

It's a strange family to have found and to hold to, but even more powerful to know, at last, that I can't any longer stand clear.

IN BERLIN

I felt smaller in Berlin than I ever had before: the Northern Germans are, by and large, a big-boned people, the shanks of their legs are particularly impressive. My language teacher had taken to calling me 'Fee-ona', from the German word for fairy, or sprite; I couldn't reach any of the pots in the kitchen of my billet. And I was nervous, as I always am at train stations, that evening, faced with the mechanised movement of so many people, so many ways to get swept up and out and along. The station was crawling with football fans headed to a screening of a European Championship match somewhere near the Brandenburg Gate, I was lost and I was late, and I knew, as it were, that the German trains would run on time.

I was wending my way west, I sat against a tinted window, the sinking of the sun slow and languorous as it is in the height of summer at those latitudes. It was dusk for almost all of my four-hour journey, only the last few towns were finally sinking into the dark. As I travelled, the window reflected, just off-centre, a glowing orange sun and the landscape passing on the other side of the train. But the reflection blurred slightly, fuzzed around the edges, the long sun tinted the whole scene the strange sepia-orange of old polaroids. It was as if I was looking, suddenly, at the present landscape through some strange, shadowy resemblance of the past, as if I were filtering everything I saw through a photo album long gone grainy and crackled. Berlin is a nostalgic city, its past still present, somehow, in its mismatched buildings and large-scale public monuments scattered across its suburbs, in pockets of people still talking about what it was like in the broken-down, bohemian years just after reunification. I never could tell if the city, at least, had found a way to come to terms with its own past, or this remembering.

I was travelling west after a month of intense language classes, and an even more intense schedule of visits to museums and to makeshift bars with ex-pat poets, who continued to delight in the ridiculously low prices and large shots of hard spirits in Berlin, and taking a break from the writers' fellowship that had brought me to that city, to revisit Münster. Münster claims fame as the bicycle capital of Germany, and as the site of the gothic *Lambertikirche* cathedral, its clock face supporting three huge, blackened cages. These cages once held the corpses of the town's most famous rebels, who had promoted propertylessness and polygamy, and had controlled the city for eleven months, sometime in the sixteenth century. I hadn't been to Münster for more than ten years, since a winter-long student exchange in high school. My host family, in the first days of my visit, had borrowed a neighbour's child's bike, a *Lottorad*, for me. As I rode into school each day, at least one person would say *Oh, I had one of those when I was small.* I had been well then.

My host parents, Hannelore and Christian, picked me up from the train with their dog, a sleek, aloof and lanky thing, with a chest that swept magnificently upwards. In the front hallway, the very same deer-skulls still hung on the walls, the date they were hunted down written in black ink across their foreheads. The same Warhol print in the living room. The same tablecloth was in the kitchen, I'd remembered its pattern of culinary herbs and their cursive names, which had soaked into me a marvellous vocabulary: *Basilikum, Thymian, Rosmarin, Salbei.* In my attic bedroom with the sloping roof, the one I'd slept in all those years ago, a bunch of pale pink snapdragons, called *Löwenmau* in German, lions' maws, were resting on the bedside table. The relief I felt was physical, a sudden heaviness of limb, an abandoning of the constant guardedness that Berlin had pressed upon me. I remembered waking early in this room and watching nuns cycle past the house on thin-framed bikes, trying to catch the first snow of the season in my hands from the small window. On the green writing desk was a ceramic dish filled with foil-wrapped marzipan. 'You must still love marzipan!' Hannelore said.

In Berlin, I couldn't help but realise, very early on, that so much of what we know medically about hunger comes, however indirectly, from this land. That the two most notorious – and most thorough – studies of hunger came about because of the Second World War. The first of these is easier to talk about, because it happened in a Minnesota university, with volunteers, in preparation for an eventuality that no one really knew the scale of yet, an academic hunger. It was 1944, and ethics boards were yet to be imagined into being.

The Minnesota Experiment recruited a group of healthy young men, mostly conscientious objectors, who had passed a rigorous series of physical and psychological tests to prove that they were specimens in their prime. These men were deliberately deprived of food over a period of nine months, and the changes in their weight, behaviour, physical functioning observed at a minute level, before a period of controlled re-feeding later on. The researchers were creating, in a scientific way, a microcosm of what whole populations were experiencing in Europe, trying to model what rehabilitation might need to look like once the war was won. At this stage, the scientists were thinking only of the civilian damage of war – the famine caused by destruction of farmland, loss of manpower, disruption of infrastructure. No one could imagine yet the scale of what was happening in the camps.

The men ate boiled potatoes, swedes, macaroni, bread, the kinds of foods that Europe's population was relying so heavily on. They were given small doses, occasionally and unpredictably, of sugar, butter or meat. They were expected to walk twenty-two miles each day, and to lose twenty-five per cent of their body weight in the first twelve weeks. One of the diagnostic definitions of anorexia, in comparison, is a ten per cent bodyweight loss. The lead investigator, Ancel Keys, became well known in the 1960s for his books on 'The Mediterranean Diet', advocating olive oil, antipasto and red wine. He also invented the Body Mass Index, the measure of relative height and weight that's still used to determine, however bluntly, any person's healthy weight.

Keys' subjects, these perfectly healthy young men, soon exhibited much of the behaviour that I had only ever seen, before I read about his experiment, written up as the symptomology of any eating disorder. The lists of things to watch for in your daughter, the tell-tale signs I'd been so steadfastly ignoring in myself. The men grew rigid and controlling around meal times and developed intricate rituals, eating slowly, guarding their plates, asking for extra salt and extra spices. (My use of garlic had become infamous within my family, my dishes inedible to everyone else.) They chewed each mouthful many times, cut their potatoes into miniscule, even proportions, sat at the same place, at the same table, every time.

Some men drank up to fifteen cups of coffee in one day, others chewed gum endlessly, they chewed their hair and nails. They collected cookbooks, and takeaway menus, became irritable, snappy, squabbly. They were possessive. One man was caught riffling through the laboratory's garbage, eating food scraps straight from the bin. Most bought and hoarded food – not to eat, just to own – and kept it in the wardrobes of their rooms. And every single one of the thirty-six volunteers eventually stole from the grocer in the town where they were staying.

I had been stealing food, by the time I read about the Minnesota Experiment, for over two years, mostly from the oversized, overstocked Coles on the first floor of the Broadway Centre, near my home. It wasn't a matter of need, I could afford the items I was dropping in to the bottom of my bag – cheeses, sauces, the occasional tray of meat. I rarely ate them. I know I felt, at times, resentful at the idea of paying for food that I'd go to great lengths to avoid, that I only needed to feed to friends at dinner parties, or to give my pantry shelves some appearance of normality. I know too that it was only the items that I didn't consider part of my accepted repertoire of foods that I wouldn't pay for – but it's still not something that I really understand. I'd said this out loud, inside the hospital, and there was only silence.

And then the other women started talking. One of them had stolen ice-cream, chocolates, in the large quantities she was embarrassed to run past the check-out staff. One had been unable to pay for her binges, another for the asparagus and brussels sprouts that she'd been buying out-of-season. Two had been caught by store detectives, one was forced to go to court.

None of us had ever spoken of our thefts before. But part of each of us had become rodent-like, gathering and squirrelling away the things we needed to survive, hoarding outside ourselves the things we kept in such dire shortage inside our bodies.

The men in the Minnesota Experiment grew apathetic, inattentive, sad. They gave up on their studies, on their relationships, because they just couldn't be bothered any more. Their dreams, when they occurred, were about food. I only recently realised that most people don't eat in their dreams.

The physical effects of starvation syndrome are much more familiar, more obvious. The body grows thin, the organs – especially the heart and stomach – slow, and shrink. Bones hollow, muscles waste as the body begins to feed off itself. The skin grows dull, flaky and grey, it breaks easily, and repairs itself with difficulty. It bruises. Hands and feet grow cold, hair and nails became brittle. Hormone production shuts down entirely. Keys described the process as a strange kind of accelerated ageing, a trimming back, the body's economising on anything that isn't essential to survival. The men fell more often, grew clumsier. But their senses stayed alert, and their mental acuity did too. Starvation is a state of constant sensual anxiety, even as the body powers down.

This is the metaphor: in the hospital, we were told that our bodies were like cars, we have to fill them up with petrol or they stop running. I said I was trying out solar power, and was sent from the room like a naughty child.

The Minnesota Experiment was less successful around the question of rehabilitation – it wasn't until the sweeping crises across Africa in the 1980s and 90s that scientists finally got a handle on the delicate processes of refeeding the starving body without causing it to shut down completely in shock. The experiment had been designed to include two phases of refeeding: in the first six weeks, a controlled and gradual stepping up, where different groups of men were given different supplements, different amounts of calories, but essentially the same meals, potatoes, swedes, butterless bread. This was to be followed by a 'free' phase, where the men were allowed to eat whatever they desired. But the men rebelled in the controlled phase, angry and impatient, and began eating outside of the program. They'd grown stubborn and rigid and controlling, tuned inwards, into themselves.

But as the men slowly became better fed, almost all of their symptoms reversed. With nutrition, the body healed itself, with energy, the brain returned to full functionality. But behaviourally, psychologically, there were traces that remained, tactics learnt that just wouldn't go away. All of the men ended the project weighing more than they had at the beginning, eating more, and more quickly, lest the food be taken from them again. Many of them battled with obesity for the rest of their lives, others claimed to have never lost their distrustfulness. Three of them left their studies to become chefs. I've met many former eating-disorder patients who've become psychiatric nurses; others, in the throes of their illnesses, working in restaurants or cafés.

The body never forgets starvation. I think of my grandfather, still keeping old, but repairable watches, promotional DVDs from Sunday newspapers, recycled pieces of string inside his cupboards, having come of age in the Depression.

More and more I think that the body never forgets places, the spaces it has moved through. I walked through the empty bedrooms on the top floor of that house in Münster, where my host sisters, now studying in larger towns across the country, had grown up. I remembered laughing with Marieke over her English homework ('I think Simon *fancies* you!'), playing card games on the rolled-rag carpet, lighting candles with Daniele and strategising about her painful crush on her hockey coach, Micha. The cold tiles beneath my feet. I remembered Daniele convincing me that the pale gratings on my soft-serve icecream, which the Germans call *Spaghetti-Eis*, were parmesan cheese, ordering a pizza with *Erbsen* because I didn't know the word translated as green peas, how I started mimicking the way Daniele would stab her teaspoon through the peeled-back paper lid of her emptied yoghurt.

Downstairs the next morning, Hannelore and Christian were sitting at opposite ends of their dark-wood table, the still points in a scattershot of newspapers, pots of marmalade and jam and plates of bread, a silver coffee service, squat peaches and crumbled eggshells. Hannelore leapt to her feet and hugged me. '*Fichen*,' she said, using the diminutive, 'we take sweet breakfast here, but I remember you like cheese!' She bounded to the cellar for another platter, more butter, they'd chosen regional specialties and a smoky raclette, which I didn't remember having tried before until I bit into the wedge thrust on my plate. The body remembers.

One of my Australian friends now living in Berlin claims the trick to a German-style breakfast is to empty your pantry onto the table.

I was talking to Christian about Berlin, how fascinated I had been by the very visible layerings of history on the skin of the city, struggling to express this in my clumsy, flat-tongued German. Christian had been born there, but was evacuated as a small child to his relatives in the countryside near Hanover in the early stages of the war, only ever able to return on short visits after the division of the country. He loves the region that he lives in, its potted history, the way its old monarchs came to rule over England. 'You see, *Fichen*,' he said suddenly, 'This is why we think of you, still, as our Australian daughter! You were always interested, always keen to be involved. You were always *curious*, yes?' The German word for curious, *neugierig*, means greedy for the new.

I stopped pushing the cheese around my plate, telescoped suddenly outside of my self. I saw the image had stayed frozen there, in someone else's eyes, across the intervening years. I got a glimpse of my fuzzy sixteen-year-old self, overseas for the first time, as yet uncomplicated by disease.

Hannelore took me to the markets that morning, where

eggs were sorted into cartons according to the colour of their shell. She introduced me to their greengrocer, a bow-armed, braided woman, and bought me a dried fruit mix named 'Sunshine' because it made her think about my home. We stopped in at a church on the way back where a group of women were raising funds for the blind, by teaching passersby to type in Braille, using a six-pronged machine. I stepped up to have a try, and the young woman in charge immediately asked '*Können Sie Deutsch?*'

Hannelore visibly expanded in pride. 'Fiona,' she said, 'is a *Germanist.*'

I'd never though of myself in that way before, either.

In Berlin, I was constantly being asked why I had learnt German, even by the ex-pat writers I kept meeting, most of whom could only stumble through a menu or a ticket purchase, regardless of how long they had been living in the city. There were exceptions, of course: the students studying Heidegger, Marx or Kant, those who'd learnt bedroom intimacies from local girlfriends. No one ever believes me when I say I love the way the language sounds, how full and fleshy it feels in the mouth, how chewy. But it's also a systematic language, bound by rules, by precise and careful delineations. It may well be that this is what appeals to me, this structure, this clarity. This regulation. This control.

It took me some weeks to adjust to the different rhythm of time in Berlin. I've always been an early riser, but this city doesn't shake itself awake, in summer at least, until close to noon. Instead, I walked the streets in the mornings, the furry blossoms of linden trees drifting in heaps around me, the footpaths uneven and cracked by tree roots. In my first days, mapless, I went searching for remnants of the Wall, traced instead the lines of metal plates embedded in the street to mark its footprint. I was barely three months out of hospital, that first, fraught admission and I wasn't supposed to be walking like this. But I was in Walter Benjamin's city, a flâneur's city, and I was terrified by the ferocity of the cyclists to boot. I took to having breakfast, once the shutters started rolling up, in a café called Suicide Sue, each day a single slice of bread with tomato and soft cheese.

In those first days I'd felt stiff-tongued and dumb. It had been at least six years since I'd last had cause to use my German, and my mouth had rusted over. I could understand everything that was being said to me, eavesdrop on conversations, but the words I wanted to use were always hovering somewhere just out of my reach. I spent a lot of time nodding, smiling my way through shop transactions, unable to participate properly in the small social exchanges of the everyday. I was without words, somehow, and I felt it all the more keenly, this slipping away of language, because I was in the city to write.

Even as I started to remember, to refamiliarise, I realised I still had to rely on simpler constructions, simpler approximations for the things I wanted to say. In German, I was unsubtle, convoluted, and anything but witty. In a foreign language I had a different personality and it was never possible to see a person that I recognised reflected in my interactions with other people. I had a massage one afternoon, and cried upon being touched.

Six months after my first stay in Münster, Daniele made her reciprocal visit to Sydney. My family's house is perched on the edge of bushland, at the point where the valley that it covers becomes too steep to build on. Besides her hockey, Daniele had always been a jogger, she was muscular and strong, and once jokingly referred to her lycra-clad body as a *Kampfwürstchen*, a little combat sausage. She was horrified by how few flat areas there were to jog along near my house, but did it anyway, coming back with the prickles we've always called stickybeaks clinging to her socks.

Daniele's family didn't have a computer – they still don't – so when she typed emails home to her father's university address or to school friends, she took close to an hour, staring at the keyboard and pressing each key individually with her index finger. I helped her out a few times, typing from her dictation, pausing occasionally to ask about unusual, beautiful words. In one email to Daniele's best friend, I'd typed her words: *Mein Eßverhältnis, Gott sei Dank, bleibt gut.* 'My eating behaviour, thank god, is still fine.' I didn't question her at the time, pretended that I didn't understand the folded compound word. I didn't know what lay ahead.

As a part of their support for foreign students, the Goethe Institut, where the language course for my fellowship was held, offered a series of cultural events: film screenings, walking tours, mini-golf. I loved the three-hour walking tours, of course, but also signed up for a daytrip, on a Sunday, catching the fast train northwards to Oranienberg and Sachsenhausen, the first concentration camp built by the Nazi regime. I was sitting next to a broad-shouldered Canadian, who'd taken a liking to me earlier that week, when we'd surreptitiously, illicitly, held an English conversation in the Institut's courtyard. He'd rocked up to our meeting point barely able to walk, clutching at a kebab and wearing lipstick on his cheekbone, mumbling something about a club with a giant swing. I was furious at his goofy, boozy grin, and deliberately lost him as soon as we disembarked.

There's a long walkway leading up to the gates of the camp, with wildflowers pressing up along its borders. I picked a small, orange poppy to wear in my hair.

Sachsenhausen is a terrible place, a fraught place, stark and bare, its triangular parade grounds open to the sky. It was a labour camp, filled at first with writers, artists, activists, conscientious objectors, homosexuals, criminals, before gypsies and Jews were added to Hitler's list of undesirables. Few buildings remain there now: the three watchtowers, one of the barracks, the morgue. The central ground is dominated by a red-brick monument, built by the GDR government in the 1960s, to commemorate the early German socialists who were interned there – the Party always claimed their state was founded by the people who had resisted fascism right throughout Hitler's reign.

Sachsenhausen was not initially an extermination camp, although it was expanded later to include a series of gas chambers. It was the first labour camp, allied with local industry. The inmates were made to walk endless laps of the parade ground to test the durability of shoes. In this camp, it was discovered that hungry inmates are less likely to have the energy to rebel.

Much of what we know about the physicality of starvation comes from studies conducted by and with the starving population of the Warsaw Ghetto during the Nazi occupation of Poland. In the two years that the studies ran, before the final liquidation of the Ghetto, almost thirty malnourished Jewish doctors living within its limits studied growth rate, weight, organ size, dermatology, immunology, circulation, fluid retention, bone density, body temperature, vitamin retention, the functioning of the senses, of hormones, of digestion. In two years, they conducted 3658 autopsies. Only seven of the doctors survived the war. One, a pathologist, Theodosia Goliborska, emigrated to Australia in 1946, and continued to practise at least until the 1980s, in this country that has never had to understand such desperate, widespread hunger.

We learn about hunger through hardship, through war or famine, natural disaster or political crisis. We learn through bodies forced to the edge, bodies that have become sites of trauma, collateral damage in conflicts, famines, persecution. It's a terrible laboratory that our knowledge comes from, and a horrific debt that I often feel I owe, because my body could not have been nursed back towards health without these studies born of suffering. I still have trouble, sometimes, recognising that I didn't choose my hunger. That no one ever does.

I arrived in Berlin at the height of *Spargelzeit*, the two or three weeks in late spring when asparagus is ripe and super-abundant, and sold in bunches as thick as my thigh, translucent white, or mottled green. The old-style German restaurants and pubs all display blackboards near their geranium beds, listing asparagus menus: asparagus quiche, asparagus soup, asparagus gratin, asparagus hollandaise; they continue to serve giant wurst and pork knuckles and schnitzels, peas and carrots out of cans. In a way, this was a blessing: I'm comfortable eating asparagus, but still can't even imagine sitting down to eat a schnitzel that overspills a dinner plate. After *Spargelzeit* comes strawberry season, and a stall sprouted suddenly outside my communist-era apartment block, painted red with a green canvas roof, manned by a beautiful, bored strawberry-blonde in denim shorts.

Along with this celebration in Germany of the seasonality of food, I realised too that Germans *believe* – the word is not too strong – in butter. Only skim milk under sufferance. Consider cake part of their cultural heritage. It was barely three months since I'd been discharged from the hospital, but I could see how far I'd come, against this backdrop. Even though I was struggling, slowly cutting back and skipping meals, if I had been in Berlin before the hospital, I would have panicked every time my bread was buttered, refused to drink my coffee if it wasn't made on skim, been unable to even taste the cakes my classmates bought in the breaks between our lessons.

On my last day in Münster, Hannelore and Christian took me to visit the ancestral home of the area's most famous lyric poet, the eccentric, ardent Annette von Droste-Hülshoff. I walked through her low-roofed, top-floor bedroom, running my fingers across her writing desk, her curiosity cabinet filled with speckled-shelled blown eggs, pinned dragonflies. Her bed was hard and thin and narrow.

Hannelore packed a dinner for my four-hour train trip back to Berlin: a two-cheese sandwich with butter, an apple and a peach. A box of chocolate biscuits, one box of pralines, a packet of *Gummibärchen*, a glass bottle of mineral water. We had strawberry tart for afternoon tea, and Hannelore asked me if I wanted cream beside it. She smiled when I declined. 'I didn't think so,' she said, 'Daniele never takes cream either, you always had such similar tastes. I remember when we had pancakes, you both would pat them down with kitchen paper. Pat, pat, pat, with kitchen paper, before you ate them.'

I didn't know what to say. I had been well then, I didn't know what lay ahead.

IN MINIATURE

I

It seems a strange place to start writing about the miniature, but I want to begin on the internet, because I found there, for a time, a thing I could hardly have conceived would have existed, a community of illness, specifically for the kinds of illnesses that we often keep silent and hidden within ourselves. I want to begin on the internet because I found there a space for grim jokes about vomiting on a stranger's shoes or pretending to understand when others talk about fry-up hangover breakfasts, for complaining about the poor quality of hospital food, or ridiculous dietetic terms like 'fun food' for the kinds of things – like chocolate and chips – that cause us the most distress. I never expected to meet, in however disembodied a form, so many people whose bodies are also bearing the brunt of a similar hunger to mine.

I want to begin on the internet too because of an image

that circulates, from time to time, within this community of illness – virally, as it were – an 'affirmation card' mercifully lacking in butterflies, sunsets, dolphins or daisies; hand-drawn, it begins with a question that seems simple, but which nagged at me for weeks when I first saw it: *Exactly why do we want to be smaller?*

I've never been tall, I've never been large; and I've always been distressed by the way my illness made me bony, made me tiny, made me small. I know that this makes me unusual in this illness – that almost all of the other people I've met in treatment can only see their bodies as huge, and hideously so, even when they're only able to fit in to childrens' clothes. And I don't want to be any smaller, not at all. But the question stayed with me, I realised, because I've gotten used to being small, and I know now that there's a part of me that can't imagine being otherwise, that maybe even doesn't want those changes, however uncomfortable and unattractive they may be, to reverse themselves. A part of me that's terrifying, and that's ugly too, perhaps because it's so irrational and seems like a desire to remain unwell when I want so much, and give so much time and energy and money, to become well. This smallness, or this awful desire to remain small is, perhaps, one of the last strongholds of my illness. But smallness, the miniature, has a profound and unsettling power of its own, and perhaps this is its appeal. It is, after all, a power that is as complex and contradictory as that of hunger itself.

From the first glance, miniature objects unsettle our perception: because of their disparity in scale, because something is not real or right about them, we're forced to look again. Like any discrepancy, especially any unexpected distortion of size, they stand out (like the proverbial, swollen sore thumb), they 'shock us into attention' as the novelist Steven Millhauser writes, in describing his own fascination with miniature things. They force us to double take: too-small things arrest the everyday with their incongruity, they upset our regular worlds, those landscapes and objects that we almost stop seeing the more comfortable we become within and beside them, the more often we move through them. Tiny things can bring us back to wonder, to surprise, to a more completely attentive engagement with the world.

But to actually *be* miniature, to be a smaller model of a naturally-existing thing is to fall under this kind of attention, this arrested gaze. It is to become something unusual, somehow out of place, something not quite right. To be miniature is to be the strange source of this shock and wonder in others, of fascination and unease at once, because as much as our shrunken, tiny bodies alarm the people who love us – as well as those we simply walk past – as much as they recoil from our sharpened shoulderblades and protruding joints, there's also a morbid kind of fascination that's always there as well. I've lost count of the number of people who've told me that they simply don't know how I *do* it. *I'd just get too hungry* or *I just love food too much*, they say.

I'll never forget that visible flinch, the whipped-around

heads, even as I know now that I do it – flinch, stare, look backwards – too. My own attention to too-small bodies, though, is tinged with a terrible sadness, and also a shameful but profound envy: things were simpler then, when I was underweight and hungry, my body seems to say. I didn't have to think or feel at all.

Miniatures, too-small things, are always scale models; they do not exist except as a representation of something else, or more precisely, as an exemplar of something bigger and less carefully-crafted, less constructed. They are not real, that is, not in and of themselves. A friend once referred to me, at my sickest, as a shadow of my former self, a thing less real because smaller, and ghosted by the larger object that my miniature self had been modelled from. (I sometimes think that, in this sense, I've become hyper-real, because the original referent, my healthy, larger body, has been lost for so long now; even I no longer remember how it looked or felt or moved.)

To be miniature, then, is to occupy space differently, and especially, pointedly, to have a different occupation of public space. We disturb it with our discrepancy, even as our smallness means we that we occupy less of it. I think sometimes that the drive to hunger, the drive towards smallness, is about precisely this: we feel so uncertain, so anxious about our rightful space within the world, that we try to take up as little of it as possible. It is a drive to disappear that can only ever succeed in making us more prominent, more visible because it makes us as different and offensive on the outside as we so often feel we are at heart.

But the strangest thing about miniature objects is, I think, the idea of their craftedness, or careful construction, an unreality or unnaturalness that's utterly unsettling because it has to be so detailed and precise. There's real skill, exceptional care and time involved in making miniatures.

It was at the end of the nineteenth century, in the early years of the photograph, the beginning of the age of mechanical reproduction, that miniatures as objects first became popular. The poet and essayist Susan Stewart points out that some of the earliest miniatures were books, specifically Bibles, and that these were first produced almost as elaborate business cards, as evidence of the bookbinder's skill. Unlike a full-sized and functional, mechanically-produced object, a miniature must be fastidiously and individually made, and the smaller the object is, the more precision is required in its construction, because any tiny errors or faults in a miniature object take on a far larger scale. I know this preoccupies so many of the men and women I have met in hospitals and clinics, who feel that the smaller their bodies become, the more closely they approach precision and perfection.

The early nineteenth century was also the era of the first jewellery lockets, and of eye-portraits, tiny commissioned paintings of a loved one's eye worn on a brooch hidden within the folds of the lover's clothes. These were miniatures created as tokens of memory or desire, worn close to the body, the scaled-down likeness of a lover capable of being secretly contained and carried, kept metaphorically close at all times. By the Victorian era, barely three decades later, the first dollhouses were becoming wildly fashionable, with sets of miniature furniture, minute but fully-functional sash windows, four-poster beds with cushions and curtains, wardrobes that opened onto tiny lace dresses for the scaled-down human figures that might occupy the rooms.

Victorian dollhouses, importantly, were usually made to order, as accurate representations of the true-sized houses that they would finally be installed in; they were an eerily realistic set stage or portrait of the possessions, environment and accoutrements ('Honey, I shrunk the kids!') of the people who commissioned them. There's a strange kind of vanity at play here, but also an accountability: because they are so small, all of the objects can be seen at once, ordered and in place; because the parts are miniature, the whole can be perceived complete. This too is a by-product of craftedness: it is discernibly and assuredly finite. We perceive miniature objects, always, in their entirety, no detail is invisible or able to surprise us, there's no part of them that's hidden, or beyond our range or reach. We know their whole. We hold their mystery, complete.

Perhaps what miniature objects offer us, then, are borders, those very things that it can be so hard to comprehend for our own selves, and our own lives. These are borders that are impermeable in a way that people aren't, or can't be, operating within the social world, and in public: almost every critic of the miniature is quick to point out that Lilliput, Swift's exemplary miniature world, is an island – as indeed no man can be. Smallness preserves, then, an interior, inviolable and precise, a private world that is steady and safe, however limited and constricted it may also be. Like hunger, it marks out something that we can control and own. The miniature is never messy – it is neat, it is trim and it is dear.

It's just these borders, this ability to perceive things whole, that Gaston Bachelard refers to when he writes, 'the better I am at miniaturising the world, the better I possess it,' a sentence that stopped me in my tracks when I first read it. This too is my experience of hunger – because it narrows the world so minutely and completely, because it causes such an intensity of focus within the malnourished brain, the world seems to shrink, just as the body does, and by doing so, it seems to come back under our command. It becomes small enough, narrow enough, for us to handle; it can't hurt us any more. Even our dreams are dreams of food. Of course, this is a false and contradictory kind of command: the more control we try to exert over our eating and our food, the more our illness asserts itself and the less able we are to operate autonomously, to make actual choices, uninformed by anxiety or terror, uninfluenced by the noise the illness makes inside our heads. We possess the world, perhaps, but in the process we are dispossessed of our own selves.

And yet this narrowing of focus, this 'detail-orientated thinking', as the psychological term has it, has been the one by-product of hunger that I have struggled most with, as I've tried to re-find and redefine my self and my life without it. Because detail has for so long been the stuff and substance of my poetry, my craft: the accrual of small, odd things, contradictory things, the things that undercut or illuminate the social world. It has always been detail that I've thought makes the worlds we write specific, poignant and, in essence, poetic. And it's hard even to contemplate that my writing, the thing I feel has kept me sane, may very well have been based on nothing more than cognitive pathology.

In hospital, this change to our brains was explained to us with handouts: *Being good at focusing on details can be considered a strength and there are jobs which will particularly require this skill, for example, proofreading a document.* In hospital, I read this and I was relieved. Because I'm a terrible proof-reader, and was worst when I was at my sickest, I thought at the time, this 'detail-focused thinking' must not be a problem for me. Because one small detail didn't fit, that is, I rejected the entire concept – although I didn't realise this at the time.

But afterwards, for months, I was sure that if I lost this aspect of my hunger, I would lose my writing too, and I couldn't contemplate how adrift I'd be without both anchors. I already felt like an unmoulded jelly, exposed to the air and barely holding together. Bachelard again: 'To have experienced a miniature sincerely detaches me from the surrounding world, and helps me resist the dissolution of the surrounding landscape.'

The scale of the surrounding world, even the scale of a

single human life, is nothing short of terrifying. Our worlds, our lives, are far too big to see the outline of, too big to find a shape for, too big to map or name or know. We can't conceive or perceive the world, much less our place within it; we can't contain its contradictions and variations, its overwhelming possibilities and changeability. But we can plan and re-plan our meals and the exact time that we will eat them. We can measure out portions of rice in teaspoons, divide apples into sixteen even pieces, we can count every chew before we swallow. With a dollhouse-sized world, a narrowed-down, miniature world, all of this changes.

So too, perhaps, with our bodies: if they are small enough, or fraught enough to see or feel in their entirety, we can be sure that they exist and we can be certain of their borders – and by extension, we can know the selves that they carry with certainty. We're no longer porous, no longer soluble, no longer undefined and contaminable; we are safe, at last.

Yet maintaining our own borders, our inviolability is also one of the tragedies of anorexia. People who are impermeable cannot open themselves to love, can't bear the vulnerability that is necessary for any real intimacy to take place. I was thirty years old, and well into my third hospital program, before I entered into my first relationship (my previous dating record had been six weeks); even then, I'd stiffen, sometimes, when my boyfriend wound his arm around me when we walked along the streets near where he lived, on footpaths lined with flowering cherries and art deco apartment blocks. One afternoon, early on, he said, 'I thought at first you didn't like me doing this, but it's just that you're not used to it, right?' and I couldn't tell him that I wasn't, that even this simple gesture was one I'd never received before. I was conscious of the people walking past us, thinking that they could see, could tell, we were *together*, whatever that might mean, and it made me feel exposed and somehow examined. One of his friends, too, warned him that he'd noticed it was never me who touched him first, and he thought it meant I wasn't really interested. It took months for me to learn to say sweet nothings, rather than just leave them bursting in my chest; instead, I texted photos of poems that might say them for me – the first of which was titled 'What She Could Not Tell Him'. I remember hesitating, still, because the sentiment felt too revealing, as if even other peoples' words might show too much. It feels too risky, sometimes still, to give up borders, because without them I'm not sure that I won't just dissolve.

But really *possessing* the miniature, I think, means more than just fully perceiving it, even more than being it, or feeling its borders, however powerful these experiences may be. We can hold miniatures in our hands. We can move and manipulate them; unlike their true-sized counterparts, we can physically, as well as metaphorically, grasp them, just like the Victorians did with their lockets and love tokens. Millhauser writes about this power of the miniature as representing 'the universe in graspable form...a desire to possess the world more completely, to banish the unknown and the unseen'; another critic, Melinda Alliker-Rabb, calls it a 'renunciation of sensible dimensions by the acquisition of intelligible dimensions'. A miniature world is at our mercy, we are no longer at the mercy of the world. 'We are teased out of the world of terror and death,' writes Millhauser, 'and under the enchantment of the miniature we are invited to become God.'

But being small in itself is not being God; being miniaturised is being seated at the opposite end of this equation. I am the cause of the enchantment, rather than falling under its spell. I forget, sometimes, that I'm not the same size as most of the people around me, that the perception that I've normalised within my self is so irregular. I'm often shocked when I catch my reflection in a dark window or see a photo of myself within a crowd and am reminded, suddenly, of my own disparity. Yet even this perspective has a strange and almost perverse power, this too has an allure. Even as hunger is a striving for control, for mastery over the world, for agency, our miniaturised bodies become things that can be grasped and moved and repositioned, little things that can be held and controlled. I have friends who always raise me off my feet when they hug me, who cart me around, piggybacked, when they're horsing about or less than sober, I have had lovers (albeit few and often far between) who've delighted in lifting me up and carrying my small body; most of them were also short themselves. It's a kind of surrender, a very sensual one at that, and such surrender, such giving up or in or over can be an incredible relief.

I still want, sometimes, someone or something to take from me the burden of being myself, this burden that I could perhaps only bear, for so many years, through hunger. But by being small I can enact this physically. I can be, quite literally, transported.

I've wondered, too, what might have driven my suitors to pursue me, what could possibly have been attractive to them in the way I looked then. When I was physically at my sickest, I had no interest in sex – much of this, of course, is biological: the last thing any starving animal should do is reproduce, especially if that animal is female; and as the body cuts back on unnecessary functions in order to keep itself alive, hormone and fluid production are amongst the first things sacrificed, and the ovaries – just like the heart and stomach – shrink. I didn't seek out relationships, because I had neither the energy nor the bodily imperative to do so, but I still responded, however inexpertly, when others showed interest in me.

One of these encounters I remember most: it was winter, and I was wearing two layers of long-sleeved thermal shirts beneath my blouse, two jumpers, an overcoat, and stockings underneath my jeans. He'd joked that undressing me was like playing pass-the-parcel but grew gradually more quiet as the parcel of my body grew smaller and sharper before his eyes; this was the man who, before we slept, folded a blanket up against the scythe of my shoulderblade, which had been digging into his chest. I was untouchable, and never truly naked; my borders were still intact.

But to move away from 'terror and death', to be teased out of their world: isn't that the kind of consolation we all want? Miniature objects don't just resist death because their visible boundaries and finite details make them knowable and graspable, but because their self-containment makes them somehow still and out of time: the miniature's stillness 'emphasises the activity that is outside its borders,' writes Susan Stewart, 'the miniature is a world of arrested time.' And this stillness, this timelessness is two-fold: miniature objects are functionless objects, they are decorations, displayed, but not used. And they focus our attention – like hunger – because we have to narrow in, to concentrate on their small form, their even-smaller details, in order to see them, and because this concentration, at its most intense, makes the rest of the world fall away. Time thickens. So too when we are hungry: not only does time slow when the starving body is anticipating the next meal, but our illnesses hold us still and almost static within our own lives. We can't be touched or hurt, but we also cannot love, take risks, or change or learn.

So the miniature is a different, perhaps more complete, occupation of time, as much as it is a different, because more tenuous, occupation of space. Time becomes thicker, heavier, when we're faced with the miniature. Stewart also writes about a University of Tennessee study, where participants were asked to look at miniature houses at different scales, to imagine themselves moving within them, and then to indicate, by ringing a bell, when they thought thirty minutes had passed. The smaller the house they were concentrating on, attending to, the more slowly the participants perceived time to have passed; more incredibly, the ratio of this time as they experienced it, compared to real time, corresponded almost exactly to the scale of the miniature house.

A hummingbird's heart beats at up to 1200 beats per minute, they rarely live for over a year. A mouse, with a heart rate almost half as fast, lives for twenty-four months, twice as long. An elephant has a lifespan of about eighty years, a heart rate of twenty-eight beats each minute. It is because of how much longer, denser time becomes in miniature that it might move us away from, forestall, somehow, that very terror and death.

This desire to move away from death is another of the perversities of hunger, another of the strange contradictions that seem to be the mode in which anorexia always operates. It is a disease of fear, or bodily terror at times, yet it is the very things we fear that it brings closer: we fear that we're invisible, but our disease makes us smaller; we fear that we are powerless, yet our illness changes our ability to make rational decisions and moves so many activities and opportunities – eating in restaurants, travel, maintaining relationships, even holding down a job – out of our reach. We fear failure, yet our hunger makes it impossible to concentrate for long enough to achieve; we fear that we're unlovable, and our disease makes us selfish, manipulative, flighty and unreasonable, makes us avoid social occasions or attend them only anxiously and disembodiedly. We fear death, and yet we let our bodies slowly destroy themselves, our hunger turn us into skeletons, with loose teeth and failing organs, bodies that are shutting down, but somehow still walking around.

It's a strange thing to remember now, but I've always loved tiny things. As a child, I had a collection of miniature bears, none larger than 7.5 cm high – and I remember that measurement precisely – all of them fully-jointed and most of them handmade, picked up in various craft shops in which my mother, a patchwork quilter, would spend what felt like hours (but how much thicker time is too when we are children). Years later, I bought home a tiny, china tea-set, even the teapot was smaller than my pinkie finger, and a perfect, cast-metal Buddha less than three centimetres tall, from an overseas holiday in Thailand. I've collected buttons, thimbles, tiny seashells, none of these things useful, none of them valuable or important. This fascination with the miniature has been with me always, I realise now, and for a long time before I could count my own body as one such treasure. I don't want to be a treasure, or a token or a doll, but haven't yet discovered how I might live a full-sized life instead.

IN INCREMENTS

I'll never know the point where my physical illness gave way to something different, something more complex, but more and more I think now that hunger was always with me, always gnawing away somewhere in me, and my illness just allowed this hunger to assert itself in the only way that could possibly have been acceptable to me. I couldn't see myself as one of *those women* – I thought that eating disorders only happen to women who are vain and selfish, shallow and somehow stupid; it took me years to realise that the very opposite is true, that these diseases affect people, men and women both, who think too much and feel too keenly, who give too much of themselves to other people. I knew I wasn't vain, I wasn't selfish; but I have always felt vaguely, indeterminately sad, too vulnerable to being hurt, too empathic and too open, too demanding and determined in the standards that I set for myself and my life.

This was always the case, although my disorder has certainly sharpened these traits. Sometimes I think that my physical illness, together with my personality, the length of time it took for the doctor to find a diagnosis while my body and brain adapted to malnutrition, were all together a perfect storm that broke, at some point in time that I'll never quite pinpoint, and left this devastation in its wake.

I'll never know, that is, where and when the ground shifted, and yet I can pin down the moment I first realised that I needed to be well. In the preceding months, a summer I remember as so brightly lit that my pale skin almost fluoresced, now that I was finally freed from feeling cold to my bones and had exposed my limbs at last to the warm air, a friend repeatedly told me stories about an anorexic girl she'd been to school with, who'd eaten sushi from a garbage bin and whose heart had given way. I'd pretended I didn't know why she was telling me this. Two of my scruffy scientist friends, who worked at the university near my house, had visited me in their lunch break on a day when I was working from home and tried to take me to a medical centre where they'd pre-emptively made an appointment. I'd refused, insisted everything was fine, had drunk a sugar-free soft drink even though I had no physical reason to avoid the regular variety, and delayed my meagre lunch until they left. In the preceding months, my housemates had asked me to put them into contact with my parents, insisting as we sat together on the steep wooden stairs of our terrace. I'd agreed, but I never followed through. I had received a long-distance phone call from a friend living in China who'd been shocked by my recent photos on Facebook, and I told him that I was just working too hard. I said that I was stressed, that I was tired, that I had a lot to do, but everything otherwise was fine. I kept busy, ceaselessly busy, going out almost every night to drink with friends and watch on when they ordered dinner, telling stories and talking constantly as they ate, but never taking my eyes off their utensils. I hardly slept, and often walked, almost unconsciously, to the fridge at night, stealing the vegetables from my housemate's boxed-up leftovers and drinking litres of tastelessly dilute cordial straight from the bottle, trying to stave off my hunger with liquid.

In the preceding months I'd been heartbroken, time and again, by all of this concern that I was sure was misdirected. I felt so sorry for my friends, that they should be so worried for what I truly felt was no good reason. I was sad for their distress, that is, but never once felt my own.

On the evening that I first realised that I needed to be well, I was stopped at a red light on Fairfield Road, it was late and there were no other cars in sight. I was heading east, back home to the inner west, after visiting my family for a dinner where I'd been unable to sit still, where I'd steamed myself some vegetables rather than share their barbecue, where I'd felt I watched the whole evening as if from the wings of a stage, everything disconnected, too flattened and foreshortened, to feel real. The evening had crawled past – hunger stretches time; in this, it is like any kind of waiting.

I was exhausted. I was sobbing in the front seat of my idling car and I knew that I couldn't go on, not like this. It still feels strange to me that my tipping point, the moment it all became unbearable, was so mundane.

But more and more now I think that these things work by a slow accretion. In the same way that my hunger crept up, inch by inch, on me, each tiny change so unexceptional and unremarkable that it could go almost unnoticed until I'd cut all but a handful of ingredients from my diet, so too did it slowly become intolerable. So is the process of recovering, of change, so piecemeal and fragmented that it's sometimes hard to recognise that it is happening at all.

After this evening, I asked a friend for the phone number of the psychologist who had helped her with her own anxiety. I perched on the very edge of the hard brown couch in the appointment and talked about feeling frantic, but kept zoning out to watch a leathery man in a stretched grey singlet prune back the flowering vines on the balcony of the next building. It was a month before I told my family about these appointments (my mother almost cried with relief), several more before the psychologist convinced me to attend the eating disorders clinic in the psychiatric ward of my local hospital. It was more than two years before I recognised my condition as anorexia.

In this time too, I barely noticed the small changes that were unfolding, the firmly held beliefs about who I was, how I felt and how I ate, slowly shaking loose within my mind. Each victory was so tiny, often so partial or unabsolute, so easily lost against the background of how many more things needed to shift, that it was impossible to track them or to ever pin them down.

The horrible irony is that eating disorders only happen to people who like definition and delineation, who like clarity and knowing where they stand, so part of the process of moving past the illness is to learn that recovering can only ever be undefined, slow and without schedule, and riddled with mistakes and mess and temporary measures. We have to stop trying to recover perfectly, that is, in order to recover at all.

These are the metaphors that were repeated in the hospital. It's like learning to drive a car. It's like breaking up with an abusive partner. Like any kind of drug addiction. Like a path you've worn into the grass. Paddling a canoe against the current. Think of visitors to a house. It's ripping off a band-aid. Living with a broken leg. It's background noise. A CD jammed on a track. A frog in a pot. A cork in a bottle. A secret world. A safety net. A parasite, a function, a friend.

More frequently I think now that our minds aren't any different from our bodies, in the ways that they replace themselves and change: something like sixty billion of our cells die off each day, and like this our entire physical selves are replaced every seven years. In between, we never know which parts are new and fresh, which are decaying, which will be the next to die. Our minds shift like this too, and it's hard to write, to map, what happened and is still happening, to chart the things I did and said and felt when I'm still not sure what any of it means. Or if I ever will, or should even try to, find that certainty.

Because this isn't a narrative of sudden healing, of epiphany or of discovery, not for me, or for any of the other unwell women and men I met through hospitals, or friends-of-friends, or advocacy, we'll all be sorting through it for a long time yet. I'm not sure that there can be a narrative about potentiality, provisionality, for what it means to try to change.

One of my friends from hospital, a bubbly and huge-hearted woman a few years older than me, tells me that she's treating her recovery as an experiment: if she decides later on that her bulimia was better than whatever the other side holds she can always go back, but she's giving it her all in the meantime. Another, an acerbic but nervy trainee nurse, says she chooses which battles to fight on any given day, which days it's better to just hold on. One woman, who was in her first year of a media degree when we met in my second admission, and reminded me then so much of my own nineteen-year-old self, has regular Fear Food Fridays, where she ate something that terrified her while watching a horror movie on her couch. She had bought herself stamped metal cutlery that read 'Calories don't count on this spoon' and 'Knife in shining armour'.

I know that at first, at least, I was braver when I was with these women, that when we ate together in hospital it seemed easier, sometimes, because we all knew that we all found it difficult and horribly strange. I still watch undiseased eaters having dinner and wonder at their thoughtlessness, their ease. Another of these women has a vegetarian boyfriend who eats a steak whenever she tries something challenging and new.

My doctors never tire of telling me that we're the unlucky ones. That in almost every other mental illness, treating the symptoms makes the patient feel better, even if only in increments. That depression lifts a little, the anxious find moments of calm. But for us, when we start to eat again, doing something that distresses us six times a day, each and every day, something that our every instinct still screams against, all of the smaller hungers that our one great physical hunger has damped down, for all those years, rear up. We feel worse, far worse, when we don't have our hunger to protect us. I never thought that I would feel as much — sweeping sadness, flashes of embarrassment that make me nauseous, unbridled fury, even something I didn't recognise, at first, as loneliness — and to feel as often as I do now that I'm without my hunger. Hunger suppresses the emotions — and this is often part of its appeal — because it is impossible to get riled up about anything when your body is diverting all the energy it can muster on simply trying to stay alive.

Shortly after my first hospital admission, I started reading medical books and cultural histories of hunger. I was trying to understand this deeper, more complicated side of my illness that I'd been unable, for so long, to recognise within myself, to know its face and shape as if that alone could pull me clear. I learned that when 'hysterical anorexia', as the condition was originally named, was first described medically, it was considered a perversion of the will, and treatment was commensurately harsh. Patients were forcibly removed from their families – in what was known, rather wonderfully, as a 'parentectomy' – usually to a convent or farm. Force-feeding was both common and primitive, often resulting in broken teeth and torn oesophaguses; and many patients were bound to their beds. Even in the early twentieth century, anorexia was considered a neurotic denial of adulthood and sexuality, and treatment involved taking frequent vaginal swabs to assess the 'vitality' of its fluids, alongside injections of stimulating sex hormones, at a time when the patients' higher cognitive functions were compromised by malnutrition, and they were surrounded almost exclusively by male physicians and psychiatrists. In the fifties and sixties, patients were kept heavily sedated, often for years. In Australia, at the moment, no state has more than about eight public hospital beds for adult eating disorder patients; these beds are all in locked psychiatric wards, the waiting lists are often up to thirty-six weeks long and only available to the critically underweight and medically imperiled. I had to fight, and fight hard, to get the treatment that I needed, and I had to learn as I went, by trial and sometimes damaging error, precisely what that treatment might be. My physical condition complicates the usual treatments for anorexia: often, when I've tried to eat a food that I'm afraid of as an exercise in exposure, I've been unable to keep it down and become even more fearful as a result. I physically struggle, too, with the full-sized meals that are a part of any prescribed meal plan. And yet I know I'm not unlucky, in comparison with what has gone before.

Modern medicine still doesn't understand the pathology of anorexia, what causes any one person to turn their hunger inward while another remains untouched. Genetics plays a role, and personality; power plays a role, and so do sexuality and family and a whole range of emotions and emotional responses. So too can trauma, and striving, belonging, acceptance, acceptability and self-esteem. All of these smaller, unbearable hungers that are starved away or diminished, when the body is kept unfed.

But however similar we become as we shrink away from ourselves and from the world, the specificity of these diseases confounds me still. In the hospital, I met a springy-haired woman who was studying medicine and found that she focussed better on the slightly manic energy that comes with mild starvation. Another, dimpled and defiant, had grown up in foster care, and learnt that if she stopped eating in a house she didn't like, she would have to be moved elsewhere. Her best friend from university, who had started with a celebrity diet and liked the results a bit too much: this woman was terrified by the idea of eating a banana, but would happily have a chocolate bar, whereas another thought dairy foods were all unnecessary and unnatural. Some of us were horrified by carbohydrates, others by sugar, others by adding oil to a pan – often depending on which nutritional craze had been most prominent when we each first became ill. Other fears were harder to determine in their origin, but equally irrational: red meat but not chicken, muffins but not cakes, rice except in sushi. One woman, who'd told her workplace she was in Fiji and not in hospital, considered pineapples too high in energy to eat. I've been terrified, by turns, of apples, eggplant, tofu, melted cheese. There's a specificity to these symptoms, to these fears, against which all of the theorising and rationalising, all of the thinking and writing that I do falls down entirely.

Yet in the early weeks of my first hospital admission – which took place almost three years after that evening of sobbing over my steering wheel – I realised that the first thing that we were being given was a language. In some ways it is a jargon, that kind of language that speaks only to the initiated, that carries with it its own definition of inclusion: there are terms and phrases like 'safe food,' 'self-compassion', 'replacing'; even 'recovery' that only a patient, former or otherwise, will use. We learnt to speak about 'symptoms' and 'behaviours', rather than about the things we'd done and the mistakes we'd made. About 'urges' and 'distress' as if they were distanced and defined things, specific and somehow separable from our interior lives. We were told to speak about 'energy density'; about 'normal' rather than full-cream milk, 'fun food' rather than junk. I was expected to learn not to undercut the things I said by making jokes at the end.

We learnt a language, that is, that had our selves removed from it, a language for all of the things we'd spent years keeping unspoken and hidden away. It gave us a direct way of addressing our disease, and a distanced stance away from it; a way to stand outside of it, and stare at it, and make it other. A language to cut ourselves clear. But I still don't know how to write about what it means to get better. Even with a language, provisional as it is, I'm not sure that there can ever be a form that might contain so slippery and fragmentary a process.

My first admission, in a day program, was not physically easy. I struggled terribly – as did the doctors – with the physical symptoms of my disease: I threw up most of the prescribed meals directly onto the table (the bathrooms were, of course, locked). The woman who sat opposite me at meal times took to leaping backwards in her seat whenever I moved suddenly. I skipped breakfasts at home because I knew how much I'd have to eat at the hospital throughout the day. I was so unused to eating snacks that I thought two strawberries would be sufficient to count as morning tea. I had horrible headaches, my stomach distended, my breasts and legs ached, and I've never felt so tired in my life. I lost weight, even though the whole program was geared towards what we were told to call 'weight restoration' rather than 'weight gain'.

In the first weeks, I tried to chat at the meal table, telling stories with accompanying wild hand gestures because the silence was unsettling and painfully artificial. I introduced myself over-brightly on the first morning, even though no one there was able to respond in kind. I was bewildered; and I kept trying to normalise the very strange circumstances we'd found ourselves in, to thicken my skin where it threatened to break. I lost weight again – two hundred grams, I later found out – and was forced to leave the program for a week.

I was terrified. I was being questioned by the doctors about the way I spoke, the way I laughed, the clothes I wore, rather than the only thing that I'd seen as being problematic, the way I ate. The stories that I'd told myself about who I was, what my condition meant, how I really thought and felt, were being pulled apart or dismissed outright; I wanted so much to get better but was so terribly afraid, still unable to let go of the foundation that my hunger gave me. I lost my own belief in the face I'd always shown the world; I still think, sometimes, that I haven't yet got it back.

In the week that I was forced out of the program, I ate cake every day, determined to gain weight by any means. A chocolate lemon meringue that my mother had made from her new cookbook, a pear and Callebaut chocolate tart from Black Star Pastry, a brandied prune and vanilla torte from

Bourke St Bakery, a brownie from the café near my house in which I did most of my writing. A baked ricotta cheesecake from Papa's Patisserie in Haberfield, the sticky date pudding I'm famous for amongst my friends. I would stop and ask to take the rest away as soon as I felt my stomach muscles flensing. I cried a lot. 'You're living my dream,' the dietician said. I smiled, though I wanted to slap her, and hard.

I was put on supplements, small bottles of almost viscous milk with a chalky aftertaste barely disguised by their purported flavours. Each bottle contained the equivalent energy of a small meal, and I was able to keep them down; I was drinking, most days, four of these each day, on top of the regimented three meals, three snacks, three hours apart, that I'm still following, even now. And my body did recover, but I left the hospital, that first time, feeling like my mind had been left far behind.

On the day I was discharged, I spent the morning group session sobbing on the couch, because I so desperately wanted to stay, I was so uncertain of myself and my ability to hold steady on my own. I gathered, that night, a group of friends at a Newtown bar, knowing they'd all insist on buying me celebration drinks. I wore a new dress that I'd bought because its plunging neckline showed off the area where most of my new weight had settled. Nobody wanted to order dinner, because the place I'd chosen wasn't cheap, and I didn't want to do it on my own, so I sat there, and chewed on the limes in my drink, and I swore, over and over, that I'd never go back to hospital again.

I started in a new job. A new housemate moved in. I bought new clothes, and realised that the things I instinctively picked off the shelves – full skirts, shift dresses, pleated embellishments – were things that had suited my underweight frame, but looked strange and lumpish on me now. I went to yoga classes, and couldn't bend and reach in the way I was used to. I kept trying to eat new things but I kept making small concessions too, and within months, I was living off steamed vegetables again. But this time I knew the face of my disease, this time I knew that what I was doing was madness, was destruction, was obscene, this time I was pushing, and pushing hard, towards annihilation. I never thought that I would feel so much and so often without my hunger, and I didn't know how else to cope.

By the time I went back to the hospital for a second admission, almost all of the other women who had been contained there with me had already been back, and one had been admitted as an in-patient to an expensive private clinic, often the only option for people whom the underfunded public system can't accept or accommodate. I'd completed an online follow-up survey of psychometric measures and been startled by my poor results, then gone straight to a bar with some friends, sucking back cocktails and swearing that I'd never go back, that I couldn't. But by the time I went back to the hospital I had spent six weeks trying to prove myself to the program directors, keeping meticulous food and exercise diaries, having blood tests and being weighed weekly. I'd stopped working and I'd spent another birthday unable to eat a slice of my own cake.

I thought I'd be unshockable in my second admission, because I knew what was going to be demanded of me and I knew I wouldn't like it, but at least I'd be prepared. I felt a deep sadness every time I finished a meal, rather than a blinding panic when I sat down at the table. I swallowed my own vomit under threat of being forced to leave the program and sat for hours with the taste in the back of my throat. I learnt that if I spoke harshly, self-punitively about my slip-ups and 'behaviours', the psychologists wouldn't reprimand me and I could all but get away with skipping meals, or parts of meals, or choosing only options that didn't cause me fear. I ran baths every evening and watched my body breathing, softening under the warm water, and I cried in great shuddering sighs while my housemates watched TV in the next room.

In my second admission to the hospital, we went on an outing to a chocolate café that I'd visited several times, over the years, with the same group of friends, stirring saccharine into my coffee while they'd eaten doughnuts dipped in chocolate sauce or brownies that slowly puddled up their ice-cream. I stared down at my cake and couldn't stop thinking about everything that may always have been possible, when I'd been so deeply convinced otherwise, everything I'd been too scared to do. Everything I'd lost over the decade of my disease.

I've been admitted elsewhere since then, worked individually with psychologists and dietitians of my own, sometimes having appointments on four days in the week, still with no end in sight. I never can know how long I'll need this kind of support, which things will shift or stick or change, and when; only that the important changes are always things I do not recognise when they occur.

More and more I can't believe that I thought I ever would be able to understand exactly what it was that I had been through, ever be able to find a way to pin the experience down when what I think about it changes every time I hold it up to scrutiny. Because the brain physically changes, too, with hunger; like the body, it narrows and sharpens and grows harder, shuts down all the areas that aren't essential for survival. So too as the body recovers does it reshape itself: the brain is physically repatterned as we change the ways we act and eat.

I've been obsessed, lately, with reading about the brain, and the ways in which it hungers. In the first hospital, one of the psychologists was researching ways of mapping and re-mediating the starving brain, using functional MRI scans to chart which areas become active when eating-disordered patients are shown images of food, or asked to read out lists of words, when every now and then these words are interspersed with something non-benign: a word like ice-cream, restaurant, sugar, kilojoule, oil. In America, psychologists have used the same techniques to try to understand how a hungry brain reacts to the act of eating itself, and have found that while a healthy brain responds to food with activity along a circuit that registers pleasure, then safety and contentment – it tastes good, it is good, I am good – an anorectic brain doesn't register pleasure when eating at all, so the entire circuit is confused. The brain cannot decide if the food is good or dangerous, if the body is safe or at some uncertain kind of risk. There's no release of the reward chemicals, dopamine and serotonin, no cognitive reward for eating at all.

Other researchers have found that anorectic brains have stronger mechanisms for impulse control and for working memory, but poorly-functioning circuits for body awareness, for the recognition of physical pain – including pangs of hunger. I recognise all of this. I can remember making my way, in the first weeks of my second admission, to a lazily-late weekend breakfast with friends, with a strange feeling in my stomach, not quite nauseous, not quite anxious, but somehow close to both, and that it took me several minutes to realise I was hungry. I still lose interest in my meals long before I've eaten an appropriate amount, they still don't give me pleasure, by and large. On the other hand, my working memory for food is acute: I can still account for every single thing I've eaten over the last few days, the number of chips I may have grabbed at a party, the pieces of cheese I've picked from a platter.

But all of this understanding falls down in the face

of the specifics of my disease: it cannot help me when I'm sitting at a restaurant table surrounded by the serving plates of a shared banquet, it cannot help me when I'm desperately trying to breathe through the spasming of my oesophageal sphincter, when I'm reading a café menu and can't trust my own instincts or lack of desire.

I can't write easily about recovering because I vacillate, each day, between knowing that it's possible, and thinking that I'm not up to the task, or that my physical condition will always hold me back. I've lived for so long with my hunger, through my hunger, that my imagination fails sometimes, when I try to think of how things might be different.

When I first started writing this essay, almost six months after my second admission, I found myself driving back home after another extended dinner with my family – which now includes an additional two nieces, and my sister's partner – along the same roads, almost empty and lined with sleepy fibro houses, spilling coloured light from their TVs onto their front lawns. I'd pulled the roast chicken meat off the bones and shredded it, flipped it underneath the leafy vegetables I'd left on my plate; and I had been relieved when my sister-in-law brought along six ramekins of dessert, even though we were seven adults there. I found myself sobbing again at the traffic lights, gulping in air, and I thought, again, that I couldn't go on like this, even as I knew that I had no choice. This happens often, these moments of exhaustion and despair, and to all of the other patients I have spoken to. There's no room in any narrative of recovery I've ever seen for this terrible sadness, this unreasonable fear, and these unmeasurable movements, backwards and forwards and sideways, towards, away from and around whatever a return to health might mean.

One of the most profound changes in an anorectic brain is a rigidity in thinking, an inability to adapt cognitively to sudden changes, to let go of small details that don't matter; and it's certainly evident in the way that we eat, or think about eating. At my sickest I used to sit at the same place at my dining table for every meal, at the same times every day, using the same single set of cutlery, to know by rote the quantities before me, ten beans, three slices of tomato. I'd plan my meals hours in advance, prepare them carefully and slowly, and I still miss this focus sometimes. I miss its simplicity, how the physical world becomes heavier, almost, and everything else falls away; how the immediacy of that physical hunger, the continual tiny distractions it enforces on the body and the brain, subsumes and consumes everything greater: sadness, disappointment, uncertainty, fear.

Now I think that it's the little things, the details, that will bring me through and cut me clear. The way I haven't felt the burn of chilblains on my toes this winter. The way the saltiness of butter can bite through the thick, sharp sweetness of a piece of good fruit toast. The ability to read a book over one full day and not be made to lose focus by my anxious body. To be able to feel time just slip away, rather than congeal into long minutes of waiting for the next meal. The single days, the single meals, the tiny victories that are all the increments of change.

In recent months, I've met, for the first time, three women who are able to talk about their hunger in the past tense. I've been stunned, each time, by how normal, how unmarked they each seemed. They are all vivacious and delightfully quirky women, a writer, a designer and a lawyer, respectively. One has a healthy adolescent daughter of her own; she ordered toast when we met in a café, so that I wouldn't have to eat my morning tea alone, but this was the only hint I had, a hint only visible to the initiated, that she had ever been unwell. One of my friends from hospital refers to these people, fully recovered, as 'unicorns', because they seem like mythical beasts, so often talked about, even if few – if any – of us have ever seen them. Directly or indirectly, I've asked each of them how they were able to pull themselves clear. None of them knew; years later, the processes are unfathomable even to them. They still can't name exactly what it was that changed. Perhaps it is this that might give me hope. That something might be happening, in increments, that is outside my knowledge, outside narrative or explanation, even outside any language I might use to try and pin it down.

IN BOOKS I

The year that I first became ill, when my physical condition first developed, was the first year that I studied Australian Literature. I was in my second year of university, and was actually studying a lot of literature, as a kind of salve to the media subjects that I'd enrolled in, thinking at the time that I might like to be a journalist. (I now think of this as a bullet dodged.) One of my literature subjects was a course on nineteenth-century German prose, riddled with novels about hysterical women, sanatoria and destructive unconsciousnesses. Yet it wasn't here but in my Australian Literature lectures that I learnt about the shock of recognition; the German lecturers were more concerned with accusative declension and pluperfect tense.

The year that I first became ill, when I started vomiting without volition, no one could figure out what was happening to my body. I had gastroscopies, barium swallows, I kept food diaries. I threw up a pH monitor that had been inserted into my stomach through my nose with my first post-procedural meal and then spent several hours in Emergency, waiting for a nurse to remove it, coiled up in the back of my mouth. I lost count of the number of times doctors asked if I might be pregnant, or how I felt about my body. A specialist asked my mother, while I was present in the room, if she knew 'why I was doing this'. But the ground hadn't shifted then, at least as far as I can tell.

In the year that I first became ill I remember climbing the concrete stairs at Mortdale station and concentrating on each protesting muscle, feeling as though my legs were moving by telekinesis alone; and the almost physical longing I felt on the way through Redfern when I saw a sign on the gate of a sharehouse: *If you lived here, you'd be home by now*, and then in smaller letters *Housemate wanted*.

That year I read, for the first time, Christina Stead's *For Love Alone*. I was nineteen, and it was a set text. I remember that I disliked the male protagonist Jonathan Crowe for his self-obsession and coldness, a coldness that I thought extended to the book as a whole. I found the novel old-fashioned and too rigidly structured, the dialogue too ornate and stagey to feel poignant, to feel real. But even then, there was one section that stopped me dead, and that remained for years as my overriding memory of the book. Teresa, the intelligent and passionate heroine — she who suffers for love alone — is working in a factory in Redfern and relentlessly saving all of her money in order to buy a passage to London. Rather than pay for trams between the ferry terminal and the factory, Teresa walks. From Circular Quay to Redfern, and back, every day. She saves money; she goes hungry rather than pay for lunch, and she walks, both ways, each day. Stead's description of Teresa's physical exhaustion, of the ravages of hunger on her body, cut me to my ever-more prominent bones.

Early on, when Teresa begins to feel 'the resistance of the body' that she's pushing to its limits, just as I was mine, she divides her route into defined stretches. From the ferry to the Law School to the courts to a primary school to Hyde Park, to Tooth's Brewery, Mark Foy's, a barber, a park, a station, a street in Surry Hills, a war museum, another park, a chapel, a bridge. This is something I too had been doing, on those late and suddenly biting-cold autumn afternoons, when the walk from the lecture hall in the university's Woolley Building to the steep concrete steps at Redfern station, where an upswept draught was always and inexplicably howling, seemed unimaginably long, the idea of it alone exhausting. I found I could will myself through small stages, landmark to landmark, until I reached the dirty peach tiles of the station and sat down, propped against a pillar.

So too did the progression of Teresa's disintegration resonate with me. Teresa spends more than three years walking, being spare with her energy and money, hungering for the start of her new life. These three years are all but elided in the book, as if no real living, no real memory-making occurs within in them. All there is, is Teresa's walking, Teresa's hunger:

When she had less than a year to go, she became very weak... She became indifferent to everyone...She was beginning to notice the noise in the streets, which increased her fatigue; the smell of brewing was getting stronger and sickened her. She avoided food shops and lemonade stands. She had found the kind of step that cost her the least fatigue, a firm lope, though it might not have looked as easy as a drag and slouch...and even when she was half-fainting, she never forgot to walk with this peculiar, life-saving step which cost the least energy...She dreamed; she saw fewer people on the crowded streets but she bumped into no one...She recognised no faces and never in all these years, though she had been bred and brought up in the city, saw a person she knew on the street. She recognised noises and smells, however, things that guided her when her eyes became milky or dark as they did occasionally...She developed the acuity of a savage, in sound and in smell.

These things I remember from that period: constantly arguing with my sister in our shared car about the volume of her music, which made my brain feel foggy but which she insisted she could barely hear. Introducing myself to people who I'd already met, often several times, at picnics or parties, but was unable to recognise because I'd been almost half-conscious, ghosted by hunger when we'd conversed; on the other hand, even now, being able to recall in detail exactly which foods were served at particular gatherings: the three different cheeses and cherry tomatoes at last year's Christmas picnic, the chicken wings, potato bake and four varieties of salad at my niece's christening, the veal and pumpkin stir-fry my mother made on my twenty-first birthday. How awful I found the smell of bacon, how I'd phase in and out of conversations held around me, unable to concentrate on anything more than the bare bones of a story. I feel, sometimes, that my higher functioning has been milky and dark for years; that hunger has made me savage, as it savaged me, instead.

Teresa begins to look compulsively in shop windows selling jams, cakes, juices, fruits. This I did too. I shopped every day, I stole food. I watched other people eat almost mesmerically. I would hang around in the kitchen whenever my housemates cooked. Teresa's hunger, Stead writes, constantly 'blow[s] through her like a draught.' Mine did too.

In the year that I first became ill, I recognised the physicality of Teresa's hunger, but only this aspect of her story, and I carried it with me for years, although the rest of *For Love Alone* didn't stir me – I was nineteen, and probably too callow, too cold and self-obsessed to understand it fully. But in recent years, I started hearing so many writers talk again about Christina Stead. Several of her books, and her biography, were reissued with new introductions by writers as unlikely as Jonathan

Franzen, or as important to me as Drusilla Modjeska. Stead died in the year that I was born. I discovered that we went to the same high school.

I re-read *For Love Alone* a few years ago, just weeks after I'd started negotiating with the hospital to permit me a second admission, and days after the National Young Writers' Festival, a four-day weekend during which I'd eaten just two meals, tearing around Newcastle full of coffee, vodka and sugar-free gum. I was still ill, very much so, but at least I knew by then the shape and face of my disease. And this time, as I read the novel, I was stunned.

Teresa, I realised this time, has all of the character traits, from the very beginning of the book, that are said to make a person vulnerable to disordered eating. She is passionate, but stymied by her domineering family; intelligent, but always striving for something more: for honour, for meaning, for love. She is austere because she holds herself accountable, she demands standards and sacrifices of herself, she thinks and feels too deeply, and far too much. She sees herself as separate somehow from, and frustrated by, the life and the society that she must move through: 'She smelled, heard, saw, guessed faster, longer more than others, it seemed to her. She listened…with a galling politeness, because what she had to say was not to tell them.'

Teresa's nineteen-year-old angst at the opening of the book ('You offend my honour! I would kill anyone who offends my honour…Honour is more sacred than life,' she exclaims in the earliest scene) I first read as out-moded and overblown; almost a decade later, I recognised this sense of grasping, this need for something more, as the pulsing bass-line to so much of my life, even if the language has been different. And it's so simple for eating, the most basic, daily ritual, to become entangled in that striving, that separation. Early in the novel, Teresa refuses wine at her cousin's wedding, and her denial immediately sets her apart. Her denial makes her powerful, and it makes her strangely sensual: 'Teresa looked at them proudly; she felt immortal. The world was like a giant egg of golden glass, she could crush it. She floated; she looked at them, gleaming.'

Teresa's hunger, and her striving are always this sensual, and always linked to love – this is hunger as a yearning, as desire made physically manifest. 'Shall I die hungry?' she asks, thinking about the passion that the cold and distant Jonathan cannot show her. But more than this yearning, more than these horribly familiar character traits, what I recognised in my second reading of the book was how Teresa's walking, to and from work, shifts, in those perilously small increments, from something primarily practical – a frugality with money – to something mostly about achievement, striving, a frugality of the body. More and more, Teresa's walking becomes a way to prove that she is strong, that she is worthy of the love she craves, that she is earning her right to make choices, her right to exist, step by step, even as she physically shrinks away. It is as if she walks her way to England, and this is proof of her selflessness, because it is, at its core, a kind of self-annihilation. Very quickly, she stops walking for love alone, for the burning hope that she might be loved. 'She was not now walking only to save money.' Stead writes. 'She was outstripping illness and failure.'

That's what hunger does for people like Teresa, and for people like me. It outstrips failure, or at the very least, it makes failure something that is contingent, beyond our control: if we fail when we are hungry, we only fail because we are ill, not because of something that is lacking in ourselves. It's a strange kind of power hunger gives us – beyond that physical drivenness, hunger allows us to hold our potential *as* potential. Hunger keeps our potential untested – and limitless – because we can never access it entirely.

But more importantly, in another of those strange inversions that eating disorders offer, Teresa's hunger is a kind of sacrifice of the physical to bring her closer to a metaphysical ideal. Hunger is a measurable achievement when achievement is usually something far more abstract and ill-defined; hunger is a constant where Teresa can only be uncertain, of her purpose, her place, of Jonathan's love. Hunger is a constant reminder of what she wants, or what she's waiting for and working towards. It is grounding, it is stable, and it can be held onto, relied upon, like nothing else that Teresa has ever known.

It's important, too, that Teresa is not the only character in *For Love Alone* to equate – or at least align – hunger with love.

Soon after Teresa's arrival in London, she and Jonathan go the theatre together, and return to his bed-sit. After chastising Teresa for 'doing nothing with herself' in the years she had been saving, Jonathan begins to talk about his university life and work:

Someone...says the relation between the sexes is based on food.
Savages only have their women once or twice a year. Their food
is poor. All that about love-life of the savages is balderdash for
mammy-pappy consumption in the suburbs. Love is an illusion,
love is food. Savages don't love. It's due to an overplus of
calories, we eat more than we need...Some of the superfluidity
goes to the brains, the nerves, and we get love, sighs, groans.
Primitive love – raw fish, Cockney love – fish and chips,
middle-class love – cottage pudding, the grand passion – roast
duckling and port wine.

For Jonathan, love is a kind of hunger, its satiation something he imagines only in terms of food. For so many of the years I was unwell, I was too savage to love, and kept all of my appetites unsatiated.

Similarly, Teresa's family consider her sick body as both caused by, and the cause of, the fact that she 'hasn't got a man'. In the final year of her walking, she withdraws further from her family, eating most of her meals in seclusion (a classic eating disorder symptom), or else watching on silently as they argue over the meal table:

'Terry's going mad,' said the brother...The way she's going on, she must be going mad.'

'Women go mad if they don't get married,' said the father. 'It isn't their fault. If Terry would get herself up a bit, make herself more attractive, she'd probably get a nibble, but she can't expect men to go after a bag of bones. Now Terry was quite beefy when she was sixteen, she was quite an eyeful.

'The brother', as he is called most often, takes this even further:

Yes, it's your fault because you're so ugly, mangy, thin as a skeleton...It's your fault. Look at your hair and the hollows in your cheeks, you can almost see your teeth through your cheeks. I've seen you bathing, you can almost count every rib you've got, your arms are like sticks, your legs are like broomsticks, it's your own fault no man will have you.

Teresa's family sees her thinness not as a misplaced act of striving, but as something hysterical, her shrivelled body as directly linked with her stymied sexuality. They are, perhaps, partially correct – but only in that Teresa's hunger is a wanting, a long desire. Although the body does become the most obvious expression of these illnesses, it is also, in a way, the least important. Hunger is, I think, always an attempt to transcend the body, to become something other, something more.

Metaphors of eating are prevalent throughout *For Love Alone*. A description of Teresa's adolescent love of reading (which is, incidentally, held partly to blame for her high ideals) refers to her as having 'eaten into her few years'; an early family reprimand is 'Eat your soup and don't be a fool.' One of Teresa's most vivid childhood memories is of barges in the harbour, glimpsed on her way to school, dumping excess fruit into the water, to 'fall among the fishes,' a waste that's particularly resonant given what lies ahead for her body.

On Jonathan's part, his descriptions of and railings against his poverty are constantly figured around food — he tells Teresa early on that he always eats at home because it's all he can afford, he conflates his lack of property, and subsequent need to work, with a need to eat: 'If I had property, I wouldn't have to use my brains...I'd just enjoy. But I can't eat and so I think.' (This sentence also startled me when I re-read the book: one of the hardest things for me to deal with, as I've moved away from my hunger, is how I still find it so difficult to think, to write, to work, after I eat; how my thinking feels so much sharper, more vivid, when I'm hungry. I know I've said this to my doctors: I can't eat or I won't be able to think.) It is Jonathan, after all, who introduces Teresa to the idea of frugality, before he leaves for London, concerned as he is with always showing the world the bootstraps by which he has pulled himself up.

Most important of all, however, is Stead's presentation of eating as an erosion, a wearing away, not only of the body, but also of will, hope, and finally, recuperatively, of despair.

When, in England, Teresa and Jonathan become lost on a weekend hike (mostly due to Jonathan's self-righteousness) and are forced to spend an evening sleeping through a storm in an abandoned mill, Teresa finally sees him for the callous person that he is. She 'release[s] him from her will' and 'the harness of years drop[s] off, eaten through.' It's a remarkable choice of words, 'eaten through', and one that seems, suddenly and subtley, to close the cycle of hunger and destruction that has been plaguing Teresa for so many years.

In fact, Teresa has been physically recovering since her arrival in London, again in those perilously small increments, helped along by her new freedoms and independence, the kindnesses and attentions of colleagues, a new lover, a release from poverty and its attendant need for parsimoniousness. These are all slow and slight changes in and of themselves, yet they somehow accrue to give her the clarity to be able to cast Jonathan off (and reading this, the second time, gave me a thrill of hope). On its own, hunger does not lend itself towards epiphanies, even though it promises to do so. The metaphysical is impossible without the physical, though hunger desperately tries to convince us otherwise.

What I admire most about Stead's portrayal of Teresa is how her illness is never made unambiguous, indeed, it is never named. In all of her years of walking, Teresa does not recognise that anything has shifted – although she knows that her body has been devastated, she never thinks that she is doing anything other that what she has to do to get through. Teresa's hunger is deceptive, and her denial is complete – and this is not despite, but all the more so because she is so fierce and wilful a woman. It was deceptive for me too: I was managing the physical cause of my vomiting by cutting out the foods that triggered it, preventing it from happening by barely eating at all. I couldn't see, for years, that there was anything wrong with this, that it was any different from someone allergic to nuts avoiding eating pecan pie.

More than this, because of the way I'd thought about my hunger, my denial of my denial, the way the shifts were always so small that I didn't see them happening, I never recognised that there might be a way to write about falling under its spell, without pinning some clear progression or false awareness to the process. But Stead manages this, for Teresa, by keeping her largely unaware of the process – although the trade off for this lack of acknowledgment may well be that Teresa's hunger, or more precisely, her anorexia, is easy to miss in any reading of the book. By my second reading of *For Love Alone*, I was simply more attuned to it.

For people like Teresa it takes so long to realise that hunger is no longer an act of will, even though it is, perhaps, that willing for something else. Teresa's willing is a want to live for love, and by love alone; it is a willing to live by word and thought and not by bread and body.

IN BOOKS II

There are books that I've had
with me in hospital waiting rooms that I can never re-read
without re-reading, too, the traces that they carry of the
spaces that I took them into. I once borrowed a book that
a friend had brought back from the six months she'd spent
living in a commune near the Margaret River in Western
Australia – there were crusts of red dirt that fell, at times,
from the gutters of its pages. I think of my waiting-room
books like this. Crusts of hunger, the crusted-over time spent
sitting, waiting, trying not to think or look too much. I read
poetry in my first frightened visits to the outpatient clinic,
after the doctor I'd started seeing, for what I still thought was
simple anxiety, managed to convince me that the specialists
there could help me restore my bony body, and to convince
me, more remarkably, that checking in there was my own
idea. I read Dorothy Porter's last collection, *The Bee Hut*,

shot through with poems about hospitals and death, Emily Ballou's *Darwin Poems*, about bodies, disfigurements and death, as I sat picking at the skin around my fingernails and avoiding the eyes of the other patients. These were poems of longing and a strange, anticipatory loss, and they seemed to fit me in a way that so few of my clothes, at that time, did. Whenever anyone walked in to the waiting room, those of us already sitting would run our calculating gazes along their body, not even trying to disguise where we were looking. I'm not as sick as her, I remember thinking, so I'm okay.

In that same waiting room, three years later, when I began the process of trying to secure a second day patient admission, of trying to convince the program directors that I was ready and able to change, that I could follow their rules to the letter, that my physical condition was stable enough not to interfere with their procedures, I was carrying my broken-backed copy of Tim Winton's *Cloudstreet*. I had reopened the book for the memory of Rose, the only daughter in the flailing Pickles family, who grows sick and hard and thin shortly after she turns sixteen. The receptionist laughed at the post-its I'd left waggling out at all angles through the book as I took my shoes off, waiting to be weighed. *Happy 16th, hope you enjoy it, love from Mum* is written on the flyleaf. At sixteen, I had been well, unlike so many of the women and men I'd met in these overheated, pale green corridors. At sixteen, I didn't know what lay ahead.

I'd already re-read *Cloudstreet*, I read it for the second time in that year when I first became ill; like *For Love Alone* it had been set as an Australian Literature course text. When I last read about Rose Pickles, who had started vomiting after meals at age sixteen I thought she didn't mean to do it either, that she too was at the mercy of a body doing things that she couldn't understand. Winton phrases it like this: 'Rose didn't mind the sight of food these days…But whenever she ate more than a few mouthfuls she vomited it straight back up again, just like she knew she would.'

That line, 'just like she knew she would' deceived me, for years, because I too knew that I would throw up after I ate certain foods – I still do. I didn't recognise Rose's self-delusion because it was too similar to my actual experience.

I've since found out, reading medical histories and practitioner books, that in the years when anorexia was first medicalised (first as a form of consumption, then as hysteria), most patients reported initially 'going off' their food because eating caused them indigestion or stomach pain. I've since learnt that the stomach contains more nerves than the spinal cord, that it can feel and agitate with all the emotions that we usually ascribe to the heart, that it's the first part of the body affected by emotional distress, or stress, or trauma. Perhaps it's in the stomach that we fall in love, that we yearn, that we become heartsore and heartbroken, sick at heart. And yet I know my physical illness is not a metaphor, that the misfiring nerves and muscles of my stomach mean as little metaphysically as a broken bone or virus. It's just so tempting, at times, to try to make it all make sense, to give a shape to my disease, proscribe (even prescribe) a meaning.

When Rose becomes ill, her hunger is a weapon, because it frightens those around her, as I was always aware that mine did, with a strange and spiteful satisfaction that I've never really understood. Rose's anger is mostly directed at her mother, an ageing, alcoholic small-town beauty, too narcissistic and too disappointed to find space in her heart for her young daughter. But it's her father's heart that Rose's hunger breaks: a gentle, generally taciturn man, all Sam Pickles knows to do is 'joke around it'. When I re-read *Cloudstreet* in those waiting rooms it was this that hit me hardest, Sam's tableside interaction with his thin and distant daughter, a conversation that I barely remembered from my previous reading:

Jesus, Rose, you look like a corpse these days. It's a crime you know, he says quietly, a bloody crime.

I get fat.

You haven't been fat since you were hanging off a tit...

You have to start eatin again. It's not a joke anymore, love.

I can't, Dad.

Christ, you must be starving hungry!

I am. But I can't any more. I just toss it up again.

Bullshit, you've just talked yourself off yer tucker. Siddown an eat some with me...You'll bloody die if you don't eat.

Dad, I can't...

Give yourself some.

Dad.

Put some on your plate. Go on...Eat, Rose...

She spears a snag and bites it in half, chews recklessly and feels it slip down greasy and fine tastin.

All of it.

She can't see him for the waterblur now, but she eats and lets her cheeks run...she's up and running for the door with it all ramming upwards in her before she can even think about it...She just wants to disappear.

I'll always remember the unconscious hiss of air through my father's teeth, the sad and frightened look he gave me as I walked outside in the sleeveless cocktail dress I wore at my brother's wedding, the armholes gaping under my scraggly shoulders, the veins raised and ridge-like down my arms, the professionally made-up eyes huge in my head. That same sound he'd made weeks earlier, at a family barbecue, after he'd told me about the varieties of meat he was going to cook. I wasn't angry about this, just sad: he didn't know how to speak to me at all when I was at my sickest, when I tried to make desperate, deluded jokes about my size. How terrible and inconceivable these things must be for fathers, whose bodies have never been political in the same way as their daughters', who can't understand why we can't just eat and save our lives.

But even as I remember the number of times I've cried at dining tables, I remember that overwhelming desire to simply disappear.

My mother too used to ask me if I thought it was her fault, if there was anything that she could have done differently; I can't imagine how often she must have wanted to intervene. But my hunger is, has always been, something that I can own, something that is mine alone, and it's just this that makes it so hard to let go of. Rose has nothing she can call her own within the over-crowded, noisy house at Cloud Street, within the family where she's become the nurturer, at age sixteen. Rose doesn't own her time, her space, her body; but her hunger is her own, and preciously so.

Yet Rose recovers. It happens in the background of in the book, as other characters move to the foreground, until she relapses, years later (I know now that this happens so often that it's almost considered a normal part of the process). Eventually, though, Rose pulls herself clear of her hunger, swimming in the Swan River and falling pregnant to her new husband, the sad-eyed Quick who grew up right next door. Even so, she still recognises that there is a 'shadow in her, this dark eating thing inside' and 'sense[s] that it'd always be with her.' I didn't remember this line from my earlier reading of *Cloudstreet*, but it resonates profoundly with me now. The body doesn't forget. Perhaps my hunger will be

carried with me always, together with the things that drive
it – my tenacity, my determination, and my writing above all
else. They're dark within me, still, and I don't know what to
make of what persists.

My second admission was a split one, interrupted by the four
weeks around Christmas and the New Year, that intense
period of family, functions and food that can be difficult even
for people who aren't ill or anxious. I was rudderless over
those weeks, still raw; all of my specialists were on holidays,
all of my routines disrupted by the season. I spent a few
days with my parents on our annual family holiday, to the
same coastal town we've been visiting each January for over
twenty years. I walked along the waterfront each morning,
with joggers and cyclists sweeping past, all wrapped in tight
nylon. My mother smiled and squeezed my shoulder each
time I ate a piece of toast mid-morning, or took a single
chocolate from the box installed on the kitchen shelf. I swam
in the surf and let it buffer me about; I read on the balcony
in the afternoons, watching children walking back from the
lolly shop on the corner with white paper bags clutched in
their fists, beach towels wrapped around their waists. I was
so afraid of slipping. On that balcony, feeling suspended,
I read Carmel Bird's *The Bluebird Café*.

 I knew nothing about the book when I chose it from
the second-hand bookshop near my house, but I instantly
loved the staginess of its set-up: *The Bluebird Café* is a kind of

absurd mockumentary, complete with a cast list and glossary, about the establishment of the Historical Museum Village of Copperfield, a recreated town built beneath a huge glass dome, somewhere above the hills surrounding Launceston. To celebrate the opening of the Museum Village, a playwright with connections to the area has been sought out and commissioned to write about the old town; she is Virginia O'Day, who first came to live with her aunt and cousins in Copperfield as a seventeen-year-old, in her family's last-ditch effort to cure her anorexia.

What's remarkable about Virginia's illness in this book is the way the adult, healthy Virginia's perspective, given in a series of publicity interviews about the commission, interacts and intersects with her morbid teenage perspective, which in turn is mostly presented in diary entries. Virginia, in both incarnations, is always eloquent, articulate and self-aware. She is a writer, even as a seventeen-year-old, and her writing is a part of her pathology, as well as one of the things that pulls her clear.

As a teenager, Virginia's writing is her only means of asserting her selfhood, her way of imagining something more than what Launceston has to offer. Virginia wants to be different from her family, whom she sees as 'fakes', and to escape the future of university, teaching, marriage, that they have planned for her. The teenage Virginia sees this 'settling down' as nothing less than a kind of slow death; writing offers her a small rebellion:

I am supposed to get married and settle down in Tasmania
forever. 'Settle down' suggests to me that I am now an active
volcano, but if I do the right things I will stop exploding
and bubbling and seething and throwing up rocks and I will
gradually become less and less active...and then go to sleep and
then die altogether...[but] I will continue to lose weight and
I will continue to write [my novel] *Savage Paradise*, and when the
book is published I will be so thin, and there will be so many
shocking scenes of violence and passion in the novel that I will
be forced to leave home in disgrace.

The teenage Virginia throws thinness, violence, passion
together as the transgressions that are her only power. The
adult Virginia recognises her younger self's desire to escape,
her desire for disgrace, but is conscious now too of the fear
behind it, the fear that plagued that younger self and fed her
hunger. She tells the interviewer:

When I left school I didn't want to go to university and
become a teacher and get married and so on. I didn't even
want to grow up; I didn't want any responsibility...I was
terrified of being an adult, of getting old and dying. I was
even prepared to die young in a perverse attempt to cheat
death. So I began to starve myself...[these] are conclusions
I have come to over the years.

There's so much story hinted at in the differences
in these accounts, so much hard-won change that really

appealed to me, at a time when I was constantly revising and reshaping what I thought I knew about my self, my life and my disease.

Virginia's hunger is always explicitly tied to death, which seems to offer her the ultimate escape from her family and fate – perhaps the only escape that her adolescent self is able to envision – but it is also a sacrifice and a transcendence. Virginia's fast began, according to her sister, after a teacher suggested that her students give up eating meat as an offering or penance for a dead schoolmate's soul in Purgatory. Virginia, alone amongst her classmates, takes this advice so far as to stop eating altogether. She starts planning her funeral ('she's made a will with a description of the flowers and the music and the prayers...What she has is an incurable condition,' her sister states). Her uncle describes her as having 'a look of saintly self-denial and smugness'. Even her name, Virginia, is saintly, but also eternally childlike, untouchable, aloof.

The teenage Virginia constantly describes her own death, and writes too about things and people that have disappeared: the Indigenous inhabitants of Copperfield, her mother as a girl. My favourite of Virginia's imagined deaths occurs in the younger woman's diary, after she reads that adipose fat cells in corpses left in water become 'suet-like' in consistency as they decompose. She writes:

I like to think that if I ever did drown and stay in the water for a long time I would have so little fat on my body I would not turn to suet. Suet is one of the most horrible substances I have ever seen.

'The body of a young woman which was washed up at Rocky Cape had undergone virtually no adipocene change owing to the almost total absence of fat in life. The coroner said "If this girl has been in the water for the length of time suggested by the weight of evidence, I am inclined to suggest she had been subjected to a rigorous program of starvation prior to death. I support this theory with further evidence that the stomach of the deceased woman was in fact in a remarkably shrunken state, and was completely empty of food." Relatives of the deceased are being questioned concerning the young woman's diet and eating habits over the past year and a half.'

In those waiting rooms, I was always thinking, I'm not as sick as her, so I'm okay. I never thought, when I was hungry, about my death because I thought that my hunger, the way that I was eating, was what I needed to do in order to stay alive, in order to manage and live with my physical condition. A doctor told me, at twenty-five, I had a metabolic age of twelve, and I thought this proved that I was fit and strong and well. In the lead-up to my first admission, I was given a letter to take to my GP, outlining the care that I would need:

In the initial stages of treatment, it is recommended that the patient has the following fortnightly blood tests and assessments: Hormone levels (oestrogen, progesterone, luteinising hormone, follicle stimulating hormone); vitamin D;

bone mineral density; pulse and blood pressure; electrolytes, urea, creatinine, calcium, magnesium, phosphate, potassium, blood glucose level; white blood cell count; liver function, thyroid function; allergy diagnosis (self-reported allergies from eating disorder patients are often not reliable); body temperature. An ECG conducted monthly.

Heart, kidneys, liver, thyroid, hormones, bones: I hadn't realised that so much could be going wrong. The nurse who stuck the ECG stickers on my sternum, wrists and ankles, in a half-circle underneath my prune of a left breast, clicked her tongue whenever she touched me. 'No good,' she said, 'so skinny, no good at all.'

But what's interesting about Virginia's invented newspaper report is not so much her fascination with her own death – it's been a part of her illness from the very beginning – but the implicit punishment of her family in the last line. Like *Cloudstreet*'s Rose, like Teresa in *For Love Alone*, Virginia wields her hunger like a weapon, against a father who doesn't recognise or credit her desire to be a writer, and her mother, who has accepted the same conventional future that Virginia's father sees for her (university, marriage, children) and has even come, in her imagination, to embody it.

Virginia writes, 'My mother is so fat. She is fat and disgusting and she is so busy doing good works in the world and working for charity she wouldn't even know if I fell down dead.' Virginia's thinness visibly and violently

differentiates her from her mother, Margaret O'Day –
Margaret is as fat as Virginia is thin, but they otherwise
look very similar. Virginia's uncle describes Virginia as
'a pale, faded milky impression of her mother' and their
destinies too are designed to resemble one other. Virginia
has seen photos of her mother, slim and beautiful, in her
youth; Margaret's weight gain is said to have occurred
in bursts after the birth of each of her seven children.
But alongside child-bearing and child-rearing, Virginia
aligns other duties of domesticity, especially cooking and
entertaining, with fat – and from this is borne her fear. In
another extract from her diary, she writes:

Were all the fat women with shopping bags and tribes of
children once graceful brides with shining hair and shining
eyes?...The dainty hands have mixed and moulded and
manufactured jellies and puddings and chocolate cakes with
fluffy cream and strawberries and hundreds and thousands
and hundreds and hundreds of legs of roast two-tooth...They
bake yellow sponge cakes called Lemon Snowdrift and cream
the butter and sugar thoroughly...for the Nectarine Soufflé
they beat and beat the whites of eggs...they make ice-cream in
three flavours and they pluck fresh fruit from the fruit trees...
Knives spread with butter things that are spread with butter
such as bread and scones and also fruitcake...Then they start
pushing and poking and popping, tossing and slipping and
jamming these fruits of the earth, these works of human hands,
into their open mouths...

The level of detail in this passage, the encyclopedic listing, is an echo of an earlier description of Virginia lying in bed, taking imaginary stock of her mother's pantry: candied almonds, tins of sardines, peanut butter, powdered milk. This too is a symptom of starvation syndrome, continual and uninterrupted obsessive thinking about food, looking at and lusting after that which the body is denied.

And what is refused here, alongside food, is the domestic role of food-giver, carer, provider for the family, that her father's conventional imagination has projected for her. Domesticated women are fat women, and Virginia fears this fate, aligning and even substituting control over her body for control over her future.

It's interesting too that Virginia specifically rejects her mother's food as 'poison', eating instead apple cores and scraps of food from rubbish bins, things that are discarded or forgotten, accidental. Later on, in Copperfield, Virginia puts her problem simply: 'The trouble is, I am a girl.' She realises, in what becomes something of a refrain for her adult self, that the 'trap' she is in is the trap of 'her own nature', her gender, and the expectations that come with it.

Virginia is finally sent away to stay with her cousins Bedrock and Carrillo Mean in Copperfield after she refuses to go to a family picnic in the Launceston Gorge (constantly referred to simply as 'the Gorge', in a beautifully perverse pun). Her excuse is that she is too weak to attend, that her hunger makes her as unable as she is unwilling to participate in the rituals of her family. But instead of staying in bed, she takes a bath and admires her protruding bones, she makes herself vomit as she imagines her family eating together at their picnic, and she walks to the cemetery to continue writing her novel. Her absence is discovered when her father returns to the house early, and his anger and confusion lead to the decision to send her to the country for a 'spell'. Virginia's writing and her hunger are the paired catalysts for her removal from her family; they hold her clear, and finally bring about the physical, as well spiritual separation from her parents that she craves.

It is in the strange town of Copperfield that Virginia really begins to struggle, both with her loneliness and isolation, and with the fear that comes when her patterns of eating are threatened and disturbed. Virginia's uncle in particular is unyielding and unsympathetic to her hunger – he comments at meal times about people watching their figures and looks at Virginia as she eats, close to tears. But she continues to write, and her first diary entry from the town reads:

I am sad and lonely and I am very far from home. Today
I have eaten nothing... Here with my aunt and cousins it
will be different, and I will have to work out some different
tricks...I escaped to my room without any dinner; I said I was
too tired out from travelling. Tomorrow I must look for some
scales in the bathroom.

I remember this from the hospital, the exposure of sudden transparency, a doctor sitting at the head of the table at every meal, coaching us on: just put a bit on your fork, they'd say, take some deep breaths, remember why you're doing this, I need you to take another bite. I remember the horror when I realised, at the first meal, that the only way out was to eat it and eat it all, that none of my tricks would work here, that I was on my own, without my hunger. I remember clutching my stomach on the couch after each meal.

In Copperfield, Virginia spends most of her time in the library, writing in her notebook and reading Dickens. She is left alone, that is, for the very first time, to do just as she pleases, to be imaginative and unconstrained, and to satisfy her craving for stories, for art, for something beyond the world she knows. It is in the library that Virginia has her most important revelations about her disease; and it is in the library, surrounded by books, that she begins to eat again.

In the library, Virginia first eats under the soft duress of obligation, when her aunt brings her a biscuit and cup of tea, and stays to talk about Dickens. Virginia nibbles away at the edges of the biscuit until the whole thing disappears without her realising it, although she does feel scruitinised and watched the entire time. It's a small act of surrender, but not a simple one, and it's certainly not final. Describing the incident in her journal, Virginia is caustic and sarcastic, and it's this description that has made the book so important to me now. Virginia imagines her uncle watching her eat her biscuit, minutely, slowly, hidden in a compartment in the library wall:

He lurks in the secret place behind the wall until I have eaten the whole biscuit and then he rushes down to the Palace and shouts to all the people that the fast has been broken; the drought has ended; the rivers will flow in the parched and searing desert; the princess has laughed; the sin is original, the niece will toe the line.

This description delights me because it's such a beautiful negation of so many portrayals of recovery from eating disorders that I've read or seen, where the hungry woman suddenly decides that she'll start eating again, suddenly comes to the table, as it were, and breaks the fast. I watched the first season of the BBC drama *Skins* with my housemates in my first sharehouse; an early episode centres on the anorexic Cassie, after her last day in a private eating disorders clinic. There's a wonderful scene where she demonstrates to a friend precisely how she fooled people into thinking she was eating, mixing her food around on her plate, waving her cutlery and talking non-stop, distracting attention from the meal that she's not eating. This I recognised. But the episode ends with Cassie sitting in a diner, taking a breath, and biting into a burger. She doesn't cry. She doesn't pick the bun apart. Her hands don't shake. We don't see her shrunken stomach aching afterwards, her overwhelming need to sleep, the sadness that sweeps over her when the meal has been endured. It's as if a switch simply needs to be flicked to turn the illness off, a tablet taken to cure the infection. But even as a teenager, Virginia knows this is not the case. She knows she has to dig her own way out of the trap that is a part of her very self.

It is in the library too where Virginia realises exactly what it is that she needs to do. Writing in her notebook, she remembers seeing a doll that once belonged to Elizabeth Batman, the daughter of the founding father of Melbourne, on display in a museum. The doll, she remembers, had become an object as impersonal as any other artefact, removed from its world and its purpose. In her first direct and conscious statement about her hunger and her writing, and the links between them, she writes:

Dear Diary, I feel like a doll...I feel like the doll in the glass case with the harpoon gun and the revolver. And I believe I have realised, dear Diary, that my way out of the glass case, my way out of the trap, is through writing...I will learn to use words like tempered steel to cut my way out....if I can't get out of my own glass coffin, through my own forest, I would rather be dead.

I sometimes think that this is all I'm doing, trying to use words to cut my way out of the trap. They're not enough, but they are the strongest steel I have.

Virginia's recovery is not outlined in *The Bluebird Café*, but it is present in the space between the voices and perspectives of the character at different ages. The adult Virginia can illuminate the thoughts behind her teenage counterpart's writings, the voice that's being suppressed alongside the appetite, and we're left to notice what has shifted, what has changed. This is most powerful, when the adult Virginia describes her time in Copperfield, in the library, as the time when she recognised the symbolic value with which she had inadvertently burdened food. She describes a local boy, Jack Fisher, coming to visit her in the library with produce from his family's farm:

He tempted me with apples...lovely little red apples that looked so sweet and crisp. In the end I started eating them...Jack somehow changed my outlook...and made me take the simple way out which was to start being honest about what I wanted, I started by eating the apple I wanted to eat, and then, after quite some time, you understand, I was able to explain to my aunt and then to my father that I wanted to be a writer.

'After quite some time, you understand,' is such a small moment of qualification, but one that makes all the difference. It's one thing for Virginia to realise that she has been suppressing what she wants, what she is hungry for, another thing entirely to be able to seek it out, to give herself permission to incorporate it into her life and her body. The average time for a recovery from an eating disorder is said to be seven years – the same length of time it takes for all of the cells in a human body to be replaced.

And as with Rose, hunger leaves its shadow on Virginia, her body never forgets. It is the legacy of Virginia's teenage hunger, her obsession with disappearance and death that guides her choice of subject matter for her play about Copperfield. She has been given free scope in her commission, but her interest is held by the now-mythic story of Lovelygod Mean, who disappeared from her bed one night, aged ten, never to be seen again. Lovelygod is thought of with the same measure of speculation and fascination as the equally fictional Miranda from *Picnic at Hanging Rock* – and she is certainly another incarnation of the almost archetypal Australian legend of the missing child.

But Lovelygod also represents another version of the narrative the teenage Virginia was trying to construct for herself through her hunger: the girl who will never grow up, whose body has become a thing of mystery, a thing that disappears, never to be found. I think it is this that the adult playwright finds haunting in the story, this act of disappearance that obsessed her younger self for so long.

What writing offers Virginia, above all else, is as a way to shape her self and her experiences, especially as a teenager, when the only other way she had to do this is through her body, and her body's own extremity. I know that writing has always been the only thing, besides my hunger, that helps me make sense of the world, to find patterns and connections and with them, some kind of solidity or definition; it is also a kind of striving, a reaching for something more. Writing has always been the thing that allows me to voice what is too difficult to speak.

But even so, I resisted, for a very long time, ever writing about my illness – although my doctors had been encouraging me to do so, even from the outset of my treatment. I didn't want to write about myself, least of all about my vulnerabilities, I didn't want to be exposed or to expose the thing I thought was ugliest within me, I didn't want to show it to myself. Even the poems I wrote while I was ill are sometimes strangely disembodied – my writing group often pointed out that there was no self within them, but I didn't know how to do things otherwise, didn't want to show too much. What there was, instead, was detail, and other peoples' voices, a focus on the world around me, but never my place within it.

I realise now this was, at least in part, probably tied to my pathology: the last hospital I attended was headed by a doctor who believes that at the root of all anorexia is a fear of vulnerability, of intimacy, of the possibility of rejection; a fear that we allay by making ourselves impermeable and untouchable, unimpeachable in our hunger.

But when I did begin to write about my hunger, I was flooded with both apprehension and an intense exhilaration. Unlike Virginia, whose writing always centres on disappearance, for me, writing about my hunger demanded that it be seen. And because hunger thrives on secrecy, on that private, inviolable inner world (the very thing that makes it so appealing to Rose Pickles), it is less potent when it is public.

IN GROUP

There are some conversations that you shouldn't have with your mother, especially if you are a poet, and especially if you are a poet four months into your third stint of group therapy.

I had arrived a little early to the café where my mother and I sometimes meet for a mid-week breakfast — anxiety always lends itself to punctuality — across the road from her Ultimo office and a crisp, half-hour walk from my home. I still always order the same thing, and eat it a bit too slowly, and we still sometimes argue about whether my coffee should be made on skim milk or full cream, but we both know that barely two years ago even turning up at all would have been impossible for me. I was reading as I waited, curled up at a corner table, and when my mother arrived she asked:

'What's that you're reading?'

'It's a novel I found. By a poet, about group therapy.'

My mother turned the book over – away from the bespectacled and magnificently bearded man scowling on the front cover – to read the blurb on the back.

'It's unfinished?' She looked at me. 'Did he decide it was too hard to write? Or that he shouldn't write about the other people in the hospital?'

My mother is the only member of my family with whom I talk about my writing; we've spoken about how strange and difficult it has been, at times, to write about my illness. I hesitated before answering:

'He threw himself off a bridge.'

The book is John Berryman's *Recovery/Delusions*. There's something maddeningly perfect about that title, something that sits right at the heart of the problem of the brain, the knots it can tie itself into through illness, or when trying to come back from it: it's so hard to tell, sometimes, how much of my thinking has recovered, how much is still deluded. Untangling these knots, untying recovery from delusion, is always a messy, tentative process, and one that may well lead to other snarls – new problems, new confusions – as it progresses. How can we ever know, after all and at any time, how much of our own mind is rational, how much is operating in the fantastical, the mad? At what point does imagination tip into self-deception, at what point does narrative slip from being the best system we have for making sense of the world into sheer delusion? When is it, that is, that the mind takes on a mind of its own?

A different American poet, Wallace Stevens, puts it like this:

The mind has added nothing to human nature. It is a violence from within that protects us from a violence without. It is the imagination pressing back against the pressure of reality.

He adds that poetry is simply the expression of the mind, this violence within, which is why it 'has something to do with self-preservation', why it 'helps us to live our lives'. But even in this formulation, the imagination, as it presses back, sounds remarkably similar to delusion.

The psychiatrist in charge of the clinic where I was admitted for my third stint as a day patient, loves poetry, thinks metaphor might cure us all, would quote Walt Whitman at every opportunity. 'You are large, you contain multitudes,' he'd say to a room full of bony women, many clutching cushions in front of their stomachs, some so underweight that the outlines of their teeth were visible through their cheeks. 'You contain multitudes,' he'd say; and 'there will never be any more perfection than there is now.'

I only realised later that Berryman's unfinished novel is actually only titled *Recovery. Delusions* is the title of his last collection of poems, and in the edition I have the two works are published together, as if in composite they might offer some kind of complete – and completely morbid – picture of the poet's mind in his last days. I can't pretend that for me this isn't part of its appeal.

John Berryman began writing *Recovery* in 1970, a year in which he was hospitalised four times for alcoholism. His first hospitalisation occurred in 1958, and not one of the remaining twelve years of his life passed without at least one readmission. Nonetheless, he continued to write, and to teach, often giving lectures while on short passes from various hospitals and rehab programmes. His best-known work, the Pulitzer-Prize-winning *Dream Songs*, was written during this period; my favourite line from this work is 'my psychiatrist can lick your psychiatrist'.

The main character in *Recovery* is Alan Severance, an illustrious and famous scientist, a man of high intelligence, creativity, and rigour, at times as severe as his Dickensian name suggests. He is, of course, a fictional stand-in for Berryman – it is impossible to read him otherwise, especially as the novel's epigraph states, 'The materials of this book... especially where hallucinatory, are historical; all facts are real; ladies and gentlemen, it's true.'

There's something wonderfully appealing about the concept of an historical hallucination.

The novel opens with Severance's admission (his third, too) to Ward W of an unnamed psychiatric hospital, determined this time to 'submit' to the program, to dry out and straighten out and 'find out what the *hell* [is] wrong and fix it'. And this means group therapy. As a 'Repeater', to use the novel's terminology, Severance has to participate in both Group and mini-Group therapy sessions, all of which are run according to the precepts and structures (and with the strange jargon) of Alcoholics Anonymous, an organisation to which Berryman had, by 1971, held a membership for more than a decade.

There's no Anorectics Anonymous. This is perhaps fitting, because the disease is so often bound up with a desire for anonymity, even though, perversely enough, the body becomes increasingly conspicuous as it grows ever more extreme. It's so often, for so many, a whittling away of a self that feels intolerable, or somehow offensive: too big, too loud, too demanding, somehow too much. Part of recovering from the disease, then, is reclaiming an ego – reclaiming a sense of, and space for, the self and all its inconsistencies and imperfections.

Nonetheless, the addiction model pioneered by Alcoholics Anonymous is often touted as a method of treatment for eating disorders, especially in the US, and especially in private practice. Because hunger is – and certainly was for me – addictive; because it sharpens the senses and it numbs pain; because hunger, when it's chronic, feels so good. And like compulsive drinking, hunger happens in secret, and thrives on deception, and it cuts us off from the social world. There's even evidence that the changes it wreaks on the brain's structure are eerily similar to those caused by more obvious substance addictions.

According to the addiction model, the first step towards recovery is admitting powerlessness over the substance, over the disease: admitting that 'our lives have become unmanageable'. Yet this powerlessness is one of the biggest ironies of anorexia, one of the hardest things to admit to. Anorexia is driven, at least in part, by a desire for control or predictability – a desire to assert some kind of silent and horrible power, even as the completeness with which it takes over, with which it shuts down possibilities and circumscribes day-to-day life, is incredible.

At my sickest I worked mostly from home, to avoid eating lunch with my colleagues. I spent hours preparing salads and vegetable dishes before any picnic or party or family gathering so that there'd be something there that I felt comfortable eating, and my avoidance of the usual chips and dips and cheeses would be less obvious. I went out almost every evening so I'd be too busy to have dinner; my concentration was so fragile that I had difficulty driving. Even now, I'm nervous travelling out of range of my routines and support. Even now, I struggle to accept the advice of my doctors, because it feels as though handing over that control – the structure and regulation of my illness – means free-falling. I still don't know what it means to exist within the everyday chaos of the world, without disintegrating entirely.

And yet I know that my life had become unmanageable, that I was never in control of my hunger, that it grew stronger and more acute the more I denied that it existed.

I realise that it may well have been the unmanageability of my own young confusion, insecurity and sadness, alongside the unmanageability of my unusual and uncomfortable disease, that led me to hunger in the first place, whenever it was that the ground shifted. That violence from within pressing back against the violence of the world.

Recovery is not a linear novel. (Recovery is not a linear process.) As well as having those strange gaps and the abrupt ending that is common in unfinished books that somehow find their way to publication, it is episodic, and it is interwoven with small sections of the journal that Severance keeps throughout his hospitalisation. This is where he most directly tries to understand his problem, his own personality, his progress – or otherwise – through the twelve steps of the program. This is largely where he struggles with Step Four: make a searching and fearless inventory of the self, and the related Step Ten: continue to take personal inventory and when wrong, admit it promptly. In his journal, Severance guesses and second-guesses at the causes of his drinking, the failings of his personality, what he needs to address to get better. The logical narratives he constructs continually morph and change: from recovery to delusion and back again.

These journal entries are remarkable because Severance always believes what he is writing: in one entry he states, triumphantly, '*All* has pointed HERE'; in the next, 'Humbled (I hope) and shook...ill, deluded' and 'whether I've made any progress at all I don't know'. He writes long, interwoven explanations of his faith, his father's suicide, his overly-forgiving mother, his promiscuity, his childhood, his children, his work; each time working out a narrative whereby that particular issue lies at the heart of his addiction. Each of these narratives is logical, each chain of cause-and-effect makes perfect sense, until Severance's mind digs up something new and recasts what came before as mere delusion. It's a disorienting process to follow, and to follow in such a raw state. It's blackly humorous too (at one point, Severance becomes convinced his salvation lies in converting to Judaism), but most of all, it's terrifying for the unmoored, grasping despair it evokes in him. 'For Christ's sake,' Severance writes, 'tell me whether this belief of mine is real, and whether I can depend on at least *it*. I *am* a dependent man, I need something.'

'The terror is real,' a long-recovered friend wrote to me last year, and I've held this close since. My illness terrifies me, and so does the prospect of getting better, because I don't know where I stand without it. But more intensely, and more frequently, I know that delusion terrifies me too. Delusion horrifies me, because I know how insidious and complete a process it can be. When I first sought treatment, it was simply for anxiety, because I genuinely believed that anxiety was the only problem that I had; I believed that the way I was eating, while by no means normal, was no more unusual than a coeliac not eating bread, a diabetic monitoring their sugar. Anxiety is, in fact, the brain's normal and functional response to the threat of acute hunger, as well as the most common co-morbidity to disordered eating. I was so unwell that I only escaped forced hospitalisation because an administrator miscalculated my BMI, but I was also so deluded that I still thought, even at that point, that I was fine.

At one point in Group, Severance reads aloud from his journal, telling his fellow-patients, 'I have lately given up the words "sincerely" and "honestly", as mere con-words designed by my diseased brain to support its lying products.' He recognises and acknowledges how utterly convincing delusion can be, but ultimately qualifies even this, adding, 'So I won't say this is a sincere attempt – though, friends, *it is*.'

I love the paradox of this last sentence because it points towards a different kind of truth, a different kind of thinking – one that is at once sincere and diseased, as well as something in between. A kind of thinking that is the best the imagination can do, for now, to deal with the pressure of a reality that is equally as uncertain as it is inconstant.

Severance is, after all, a scientist – someone who, like a poet, is driven to find patterns in the world, to make ultimate sense of himself and his surroundings, to find meaning. Even if the systems and languages that scientists and poets use are vastly different, the impulse is the same. It is this very striving for sense that lends itself so easily to delusion. Writing and science are perhaps each, in themselves, a peculiar form of madness.

In one group session, Severance is asked by a facilitator, 'Alan, what sort of fellow do you see yourself as being?' and the only answer he can give is this: 'Well, I do science. Write books, lectures and so on. Sometimes I give seminars…serve on boards, train younger men. Various things.'

The facilitator replies, 'I didn't ask what you do, I don't give a damn what you do. I asked what you are.' And Severance is lost, for once, for words.

When I first read this exchange I was shocked, because it so closely mirrored one that I'd had in my first weeks of admission, when I'd responded to the psychiatrist's request to tell him about myself. I had begun, 'Well, I'm a writer, mostly a poet…', and he let me speak for several minutes before stopping me and repeating, 'Tell me about who you are, not what you do.' I too couldn't answer. At the time, I felt I had been silenced by frustration: because by saying that I am a writer I had been trying to tell him something important about how I am within the world, but I fear now that it points too to some kind of hollowness, some lack of essential self that my hunger fills – or at least masks – for me, the same way drinking does for Severance.

I lost track of how many times the doctors at this clinic, where my third admission took place, told me that my confusion and frustration are important, are generative, told me to stop trying to understand, to stop narrating. 'Get out of your head,' one therapist told me, 'and into your body.' At the time, I countered that my head had never betrayed me as my body had, but now I'm not so sure.

Berryman's novel is most remarkable for its portrayal of the group sessions that Severance must attend; group sessions that are now an integral part of many forms of modern psychiatric treatment, especially those that involve hospitalisation. The clinic I attended for my third admission, my first in the private system, treats mood disorders, eating disorders, and drug and alcohol addiction in three separate wards, each with its own schedule of group sessions, universally referred to, here too, as Groups.

We'd go to Group. Say, 'See you next Group.' We were asked by our psychologists, 'So, how are things in Group?' These groups are fascinating little societies, partly because of the severe and strange conditions under which they form, and the intense experiences that members must share in order to qualify for membership, but also because they are constantly shifting and changing as patients come and go and shift and change themselves. And they're almost entirely invisible to the wider world, and even largely absent from literature – despite the incredibly high incidence of mental illness and addiction amongst writers. (The rates are higher still for poets.)

Severance's group includes a retired professional hockey player, a businessman who can't live up to the expectations of his family, a pale girl with a manipulative, alcoholic father, a thin young woman who's convinced she's a compulsive eater (although this too is a delusion), a middle-aged janitor who phones his elderly parents several times each day, and a man simply described as a 'benign lizard'. There are discharges, new admissions, one death. The group spends a lot of time, when not in Group, attending lectures on the physical and psychological effects of heavy drinking, reading the AA manuals (called *The Big Book* and *The 24-Hour Book* respectively), and eating Eskimo Pies and drinking coffee in the Snack Room.

All I want to say about my group is that we were not all women and that we ranged in age from eighteen to fifty-nine. There were, at times, within it, two other literature students, an English teacher, an actor, a musician and a photographer, as well as an Army paramedic, a trainee doctor, a chiropractor, three mental health workers, a government clerk, a swimming teacher, three mothers, one father, and people whose illnesses have made it impossible for them to work for years. We arrived mid-morning, left mid-afternoon, had structured meal times, and sat at a single round table with happy aphorisms written on the napkin dispenser in coloured textas: 'You are beautiful and you are strong', 'It's just one meal', 'Tomorrow you might wish that you started today'. We spent a lot of time, when not in Group, knitting or crocheting, doing crosswords, and looking up cat videos on YouTube.

Berryman's *Recovery* is most powerful in the terrible, charged moments that deal directly with being in Group, in the interactions and confrontations between members, or between therapists and patients. These scenes are short and there's a lot of dialogue, which gives them an immediacy that's sometimes horrifying, and that tips, at times, to violence. In these scenes the novel captures that strange space between delusion and recovery, the raw emotion and confusion of people desperately trying to help each other and themselves, and the strange dynamics, the strange language, of people thrown together in a space deliberately removed from the external world and their regular (if less than functional) lives.

Severance's Group, according to the psychiatric principles of the time, works by confrontation, by trying to shock people into a forced recognition of their delusions, temperaments and the patterns of thinking and behaving that contribute to their problems. Each member of the group is encouraged to critique the others' behaviour, and the answers they give to the questions of the therapists. 'You've got to help each other, and you *can*, though all of you are crippled,' one of the doctors says.

I was fascinated by these exchanges because they're so different from the gentle coaxing, the quiet but continual insistence, with which the therapist in my group interacted with us, the way we were encouraged to give advice, but not step on each others' toes, to congratulate each other for the things we had achieved, ignoring whatever else we may have done that was unhelpful, unhealthy, or downright stupid.

I'm aware that the difference may well be one of diagnosis – our delusions are different from those of alcoholics, far more self-critical and harsh. Eating disorder patients are, almost without exception, hypersensitive to the opinions of others, punishingly judgemental of themselves, and easily wounded because of the fragility of their sense of self. So gentleness itself, arguably, is therapeutic, because it's something that we never grant ourselves. At criticism, cruelty and violence, however, we're old hands.

But following Severance across his group interactions has been equally fascinating and confronting for me, because he too has difficulty placing himself within the Group, at times feeling unavoidably and inexorably different from the others, at times feeling that he utterly belongs. The problem, for Severance, in his own words, is that his 'highly developed and strong *will*', his intelligence, his creativity, make it that much harder for him to negotiate the Group, because he can't help but watch on, can't help but be fascinated by the Group and its constant transformations. He struggles, at times, even to be aware that he is having difficulty completely engaging in Group and its peculiar kind of treatment, that he can't just 'swallow the Group-mystique' as he puts it.

He often describes himself as going 'into double-consciousness', a state that I recognise well, and have often spoken about with other writers: a strange state of participating in the world, but simultaneously observing and analysing it.

It's not quite detachment – more a sense of both living, and filing away, the same events at the same time. A psychologist once told me that I had 'excellent meta-cognition' and my first reaction was to add the new and beautifully peculiar word to the list in the back of my notebook.

I know that double-consciousness is problematic in group therapy, that it's prevented me, at times, from being able to give myself over to it completely. On my very first day in the clinic, we were taken to the facility's art room, directly after our supervised morning tea, for a session of art therapy with an occupational therapist. She had unpacked several bundles of construction paper, thick crayons, pots of acrylic paint and glitter (but had not unlocked the high cupboard where the scissors were kept) and as we sat down explained to us that we were going to spend the next hour drawing our eating disorders as trees. I remember thinking, right away, how excellent a detail this would be, even before I reached for the purple paint.

But this double-consciousness is also difficult because it often means that I can't help but be enthralled by the other patients, to be drawn in by their stories, when I am supposed to be making an inventory, as it were, of my own.

I've struggled with this in every Group I've attended, often walking away in the afternoon distraught by what I've heard from people whom I've so quickly come to care about, furious at the people who've hurt them and thinking up lists of small kindnesses – playlists, recipes, loaned books – that I can give them. I often leave mulling over the unexpected reactions of others, the strangely logical irrationality of the beliefs and fears they've spoken about, the points where they stop themselves from talking, shrink back into the room. It's easier, somehow, to get involved in other peoples' stories so as not to touch my own.

This continual interaction with other unwell people and their all-too-visible sadness and confusion often leaves me exhausted, distraught, yet perhaps this is exactly how Group is supposed to work. It's so much easier, too, to recognise delusion and distress in others rather than in ourselves, to see solutions for them where we ourselves feel trapped. One member of Severance's group describes it as confronting 'the imposing and uniform and entirely unacceptable world' presented by his fellow patients, and realising that 'three-quarters, at least, of every story was my story. Mirrors on every side.' These mirrors may be that much more powerful for the people in my Group: with our illnesses so closely tied to a need to be seen, or a fear of how we may be reflected back to ourselves by others.

This experience is also startlingly similar to the one I had in my very first admission, three years before this one, when I still thought that I wasn't *like that*, that my physical condition was the totality of my disease. I used to be amazed by the completeness of this delusion, that someone as intelligent as I have always thought myself to be could think so stupidly, could participate so completely in what I know now was blatant denial. But I realise now that delusion is a creative act, albeit a perverse one, and this was the only way that I could apprehend my unacceptable illness, that violence without.

It is also Severance's strong will that makes it difficult for him simply to give himself over, and submit to the regime, as much as he believes he wants to do this, as much as he wants to 'find out what the *hell* [is] wrong and fix it'. Severance knows the rationale behind the manoeuvres of his therapists, and so he's often cognitively recognising their strategy rather than engaging with it – like me, he's read far too many books on the subject of his illness and so he often knows what they are trying to do, and is able to defend himself against it before he even realises what he is doing. Severance is, after all, used to rationally, meticulously looking for solutions; he calls it 'rigorous honest private mental work'. But rational, rigorous mental work cannot unpick delusion ('if you could do it by yourself, you would have already done it'). And Severance is accused, repeatedly, of hiding behind his brain so as not to have to touch his heart.

I can't help but wonder, at times, about what happened to Berryman as he tried to write *Recovery*, what it cost him, what he gained.

But even though Severance's will is scientific and mine is not, I know that my will too was problematic in Group, that I still had difficulty suspending my disbelief, and in not rejecting wholesale the activities and concepts we were given, if I'd read about them or the psychological methodology beforehand. It didn't help, in my Group, that the therapist wore shellac nails, meticulously straightened, waist-long hair and towering heels, and was several years younger than me – a fellow patient had hunted her down on Facebook – or that the language of these methodologies, riddled with three-letter acronyms, never failed to make me cringe.

There's a whole language to recovery, of course, with 'recovery' itself as its principal proper noun (and 'meal plan' coming a close second). We talk of choice points, emotional regulation, compensation, compliance, and weight-and-shape, as if that were one word. Mechanical eating, social eating, flexible eating, normal eating, refeeding, safe food, fear food, challenge food, trigger food, fun food. Taking responsibility, checking back into life. Self compassion, self care, self talk, coping strategies, coping mechanisms, crisis management, urge surfing, down arrowing, thought challenging, distracting, dissociating, dissembling, dissonance, defusion, diffusion, ambivalence, acceptance, making space. Writing is called 'journalling' – though I refused to use the term.

This language is useful, of course, and even felt radical to me at first, because I'd never before had a way to talk about my illness and its manifestations as something separate from my self. But now it feels like swearing: use the words often enough and they lose any power to shock.

In Berryman's *Recovery*, a therapist makes a list of common Group behaviours on a chalkboard, and these buzzwords I am all-too-familiar with: 'minimising, denial, silence, projection…attacking, explaining, humour… intellectualising, agreeing, complying (playing Group), smugness, hostility, shifting'. Severance's Group, like my Group, is constantly told to 'stay *real*' ('Once you're *real*, you don't have to be consistent.') or to 'be authentic' (but also to 'fake it 'til you make it'), to 'level', to 'let go'. But more interestingly, Severence's Group distinguishes between being 'dry drunk' – being on the wagon, but still wanting to drink – and being 'sober', neither drinking nor wanting to. Group has its own inside language for its initiates, and I know it's just for us, on the inside, that it's normalised. Only last night I did a double take when a friend-of-a-friend (holding an empty soup pot at the time) said she'd just been 'on a *Game of Thrones* binge' at her boyfriend's house.

I realise too that this normalisation is not just linguistic – in Group, we quickly lost the ability to be startled by, to even bat an eyelid at, the awful and often insane ways that others behave. I've watched women in their thirties and forties suck on the corners of blankets or the ends of their hair and a young man inspect every single egg in six different cartons, trying to select the best dozen. Most recently, an hour before we were due to meet for a drink, a friend from Group sent me a text cancelling our plans because she'd taken too many laxatives and couldn't leave her bathroom. It was only later that I realised these events would be unthinkable for anybody on the outside. But illness is a foreign country, as it were; we do things differently here.

The worst problem with strong will and its delusions, for Severance at least, is that they mean he's never able to understand how he is progressing, because he can never escape the confines that his will and delusions impose upon his thinking. He can never come to understand precisely what is turning or changing within him and his mind, however furiously he writes in his journal, and he feels entirely and utterly lost because he cannot make it, or will it, otherwise. At one point, a doctor congratulates him on his progress, and Severance is rattled to his core, he writes: 'I felt witless to hear that in his opinion I'm going strong. So much for my opinion about *anything*.' It's terrifying – for Severance, as it is for me – to not know your own mind, when your mind and its work are the only things that have seemed to hold solid throughout the slow erosions of chronic illness.

My psychiatrist first told me I was doing well after a week when I'd sat in my shower after eating dinner on my couch each night, crying under the hot water, having kept myself constantly busy through the day, as if momentum alone could stop me from collapsing. I was constantly aware that this didn't feel much different from the period when I was physically at my sickest. After a week when I'd felt skinless and spilling as I walked beneath the ancient fig trees in my suburb, squashing the fallen, seedy fruit beneath my sandals; when I'd been always 'aware of the action of my heart, in the absence of physical exertion', to use the strangely haunting language of a basic diagnostic tool. This brokenness, this damage, *this* was doing well, perhaps precisely because it was a breaking down of will. But even if we can't trust our own wills and we cannot know our own minds, it's still difficult to operate around them, to try to understand that this is not a process we can think through perfectly, that we can ever understand, pin down, or control.

And yet reading Berryman's novel offered another kind of recognition to me, as if I had been in Group, a much smaller, more interior kind of Group, with Severance and Berryman too, or at least the figure of Berryman as I imagine him. An imaginative alliance with the two men, all of us confused, and all of us equally bewitched and betrayed by our own minds. And all of us, most importantly, in a place that is unfinished. Severance, of course, must remain here indefinitely, interrupted by Berryman's death. Between *Recovery* and *Delusions*, in the edition that I have, are transcriptions of Berryman's fragmented notes for the rest of the novel, but they're not a satisfying substitute for an ending: the novel simply stops, in a suspension (I'm tempted to write: a falling) between the two states. Part of me thinks this is exactly as it should be: an unintentional but radical inconclusiveness, a denial of the three-act structure that biography is often made to fit, even though life itself is never so simply and tightly contained. Another part of me thinks that if the striving for logical and fixed conclusions in our own thinking is a catalysing force that allows the stories that we tell ourselves to harden into delusion, then Severance, suspended and un-ended as he is, is finally freed from both. It's still difficult to try to imagine our own stories in this way, unfixed and uncontainable, difficult to abandon definition for our selves and lives. But the idea appeals to me because it means that any delusion must always be transient, short-lived, and so no more dangerous than a bad decision: a thing that is imperfect and regrettable, perhaps, but which was, and always is, the best thing that the mind could do to manage at the time.

IN PASSING

I received the news digitally, in a text from my old housemate, Kat. *Just to let you know*, the message said. I was curled on my couch, twisted up against my boyfriend, whom I was introducing to a trashy sci-fi series that I'd watched in the months after my first stint in the hospital program, when I still felt too fragile for the social world, too tentative in my new routines and thought patterns, to expose them too frequently to the world. It had been about a year since I'd left the house that I'd shared with Kat, the house in which I'd hit what I now call, when I talk about it, the crisis point. Where my weight had dropped to less than it had been when I was ten years old and I'd been unable to sit still for any time at all. When I was driven, constantly, by the restless, almost manic energy that acute hunger pushed through me, when I was most completely convinced that my tightly controlled, minimal eating was not a problem in and of itself, but was simply what I needed to be doing in order to manage the rare physical illness that I'd been living with since I was nineteen – by that stage, for six or seven years. When I talk about that house now, I always mention how Kat and her girlfriend Michaela would spend two or three evenings each week knitted together on the old, brown sofa that we'd rescued from the street, eating the dinners that Kat had cooked, and watching awful movies that had them both in stitches. I always mention how I'd largely stayed out of the lounge room as a result, but had visited the kitchen after they'd both gone to bed, and eaten the vegetables out of the containers of leftovers Kat had kept to take to work for the next day. *Just to let you know,* the message said. *Michaela died of a heart attack in her sleep last night.* She was thirty years old. I'd fallen out of touch when I'd left that house, when I started trying to leave my hunger and the strange half-life that it propped up as well.

I hadn't seen Michaela in person for about five years. I hadn't been in touch with her wider circle either, even though we all still live within three suburbs of each other, even though, for a time, we spent almost every evening together. Kat had been, perhaps, my best friend, for a while: she'd moved into my sharehouse from Canberra, and after travelling across Europe for several months. She knew no one in Sydney and invited me along on all her outings. She was brashly funny, curious, intensely charming and wickedly outrageous. More importantly, perhaps, she was completely certain of herself and her own decisions in a way that I have never been and that

I have always admired. Later, that winter, she started dating Michaela, and I tried to cling to that same friendship, even though there wasn't the same space for me any more and I was really just third-wheeling along, wildly, blindly and a little furiously, as my body fell apart.

My friendship with Michaela, however, largely had developed because she and her circle spent a good three nights a week at the Warren View, a pub at the end of Enmore Road, the arterial road from which the street I lived on peeled away. I knew that if I went along I could drink vodka-sodas instead of having dinner, and avoid both empty time and an empty stomach until it was time to go to bed. When I knew Michaela best it was *my* heart that was at risk of failing, the muscle itself being slowly metabolised by my malnourished body.

I've been more present in her death, and in her mourning, than I ever really was in her life, even when I was physically sitting alongside her.

Hours before I received Kat's message, I'd been on Facebook, and noticed a mutual friend had changed her profile picture to an older photo, taken at a party in the house that Kat and I had shared. In the photo, she was standing in our old kitchen, clinking beers with Michaela, both of them dressed in mens' shirts, with false moustaches and aviator glasses

— the party had had a gender-bending theme, mostly so that I could wear the secondhand boy's waistcoat and suit pants that I'd found at an op shop one weekend. Michaela's moustache had been drawn on with eyeliner, and was pencil-thin; our mutual friend's had been made by her boyfriend, who worked in a TV art department, and was a glorious and vaguely pornographic '70s-style brush. It was a great party, I remembered, and flipped back to looking at articles about misbehaving footballers, photos of cakes, and cat memes.

In the days that followed, after I received the news, I watched our other common friends do this too, change their own photos to shared shots, each of them standing next to, dancing with, winking at, toasting or passed out beside Michaela, slinging their arms across her shoulders, holding matching grimaces for the camera. They reposted old photos too, and all of these images from years ago, from the years I now think of as my lost years, as the years I don't like to remember, were suddenly a steady presence scrolling downwards on my computer screen. I was seeing Michaela far more frequently than I had in all the intervening years, precisely because I could now never see her again.

The man I'd been curled against that night called this frantic, almost instinctual reposting, this public, if mediated mourning, a digital ritual; he compared Facebook's wall to a wailing wall, against which my friends were lamenting, crying out their loss and pain. Our generation has no real rituals for grief, no way of publicly acknowledging private loss. But now we grieve as a community, because we are part of a community that exists which is expressed online, and also because it is more vital, more important, than traditional family for Michaela and for so many of our common friends.

There's an uncanny aspect to this too, of course — these rituals are only possible because of the data that the site itself has stored, the documentation of so many of the small events and interactions that make up a life, in all its minute and mundane glory. My friends were sifting through these, digging out those tiny, routine gestures that we come to love in other people, and putting them back on display. Facebook was a mausoleum, or the accident site where they were placing their own small memorials. Photographs of particular expressions, a lifted eyebrow and sardonic grin. Recordings of mock-manic dance moves. Screen grabs of text message exchanges (*Wanna come to Centrelink with me on Valentine's Day? I'll buy you a beer and we'll call it a date.*) This, they were saying, this is what I've lost, what I will miss. These are the things that I loved.

And it seems that I am the only one who does not want to remember those days.

One of the first reposted photographs of Michaela that I saw was taken in the Domain, during one of the public festival performances held there in the long evenings of summer, a close shot of three faces, Kat's, Michaela's, my own, all of us big-grinned and quite obviously tipsy. I'm wearing a pair of over-sized earrings that I loved, and that I lost some months

later when I loaned them to an absent-minded friend, and
a bright red jumper that doesn't hide the ridges of my
collarbones. I remember those summer concerts; we'd always
take picnics of cheeses, chicken, dips and bread, the pre-mixed
sugar-free vodka cruisers I drank at the time, the occasional
Scrabble board, once, a fondue pot. I'd almost always end up
eating something that I knew I couldn't, and throwing up in
the line for the portaloos that never moved quickly enough
for me to hold my troublesome stomach at bay. I clicked on
the photo, to see it in closer detail, and accidentally opened
up Michaela's own, still active, Facebook page. No one, it
turns out, knows her password. No one can shut it down.

Many of the photos that were suddenly recirculating were
photos of Michaela at the pub, her local, close to Kat's and
my house, but also halfway between Michaela's flat on the
edge of Stanmore and the townhouse halfway to Marrickville
that her best friend Naomi shared with two friends and an
ancient, bedraggled dog. I don't know how many hours I spent
there too, sitting in the beer garden that's the backdrop to
these photos, in those strange and vaguely hazy months at
the height of my illness. My own face, smiling wildly under
dead-fish eyes and sheenless skin or staring absently at the
drink in my hands, recurs again and again, near the edges of
so many of these photos.

I was unsettled by this too because I had stopped going
to the Warren View. When I started moving away from

Kat and Michaela, and began the long and awful process of distancing myself from the illness that had come to dominate each day of my life, I moved to a new house, with new places and venues in its orbit. I clung to different friends, with whom I could talk, however cautiously, about unspecified sadnesses and anxieties, and with whom, sometimes, I convalesced. I hadn't been to the Warren View for more than five years, until a few months before Michaela died, on Anzac Day. I went back, almost by accident, to meet up with another friend, a new friend, a young woman I met in the day program of the private psychiatric hospital in Western Sydney where I had my third admission; she was playing a few rounds of two-up at the pub before moving on to a bar that we'd be planning to try out together.

I walked up to the Warren View after eating my lunch at home, and sat again in that leafy garden with my friend and her strange assortment of companions – a colleague, a uni friend, an Army doctor, a soccer teammate, several of their partners. I had a drink and chatted and realised that I was no longer on edge, no longer sprung with that reckless energy that I was used to feeling in that place. I watched my new friend flirt and knock back gin-and-tonics, talk constantly and frantically, laugh with a tossed-back head at jokes that weren't really that funny. I watched her steadfastly ignore the bowls of crisps that the boys bought for the table over the hours. She bought me another drink after I'd said that I didn't want any more; in the late afternoon I asked if she'd had lunch and she replied, with obvious evasion and a vague hostility, that she'd been out for breakfast with her friends.

I watched her behave, that is, almost exactly as I used to, when I was desperate to push away my illness, when I was frantically trying to find a shape for myself, to hold myself together by clinging to the structures of other peoples' lives, when I moved around with Michaela and her circle. But I felt, that day, like I made a different peace with the place, and that by coming back to the Warren View I was able to see myself again, how much I'd changed, regardless of how much I'd lost, across the years, to my disease.

I didn't ask Kat for the details of Michaela's funeral, partly because I was unsure of the etiquette around it, partly because I didn't feel that I'd belong there, surrounded by our common friends who'd still been so deeply involved in her life, even though I'd moved away. But I kept watching Facebook, and eventually I saw a new series of posts: photographs taken in the backyard of Naomi's townhouse, unchanged in the golden afternoon light that I love in late autumn, that time of year. Our common friends playing frisbee on the tiny lawn, clutching longnecks and sitting on the wooden benches that line the fence, toasting the camera with raised eyebrows. The captions all tagged '...with Michaela Collins', even though she wasn't there, even though the photographs could never have been taken if she had been.

I wasn't there, but had been in Naomi's backyard so

many times in those months of acute illness, in that space too, alongside that circle of people. And looking at those images, from my bedroom, I still felt close to them, drawn into their common loss, a participant in their mourning every bit as vicarious, perhaps, as I had been when I sat beside them in that pub. Presence, just like connection, is always relative, and all that digitisation has done is blur lines that were never as clean-cut as we'd like to imagine. Loss a complex, multivalent thing: I know I'm mourning myself as much as I'm mourning Michaela, and the way our lives were tied together for a time.

IN HINDSIGHT

IN HINDSIGHT

'It begins quietly
in certain female children'
LOUISE GLÜCK, 'Dedication to Hunger'

I resisted, for a long time, reading any anorexia memoirs, even though I'd been reading about the condition in fiction and textbooks. Partly, I think, this is because of my time as an editor — I'd read so many badly-written pieces of 'sick lit', as I once heard the genre called, that I didn't think I'd find anything there besides excoriating descriptions of self-hatred and self-harm, all laid out in excruciating detail. Partly too, we were warned against such stories in the first hospital program that I attended. One of the psychologists there had curled her lip when another patient mentioned reading Portia de Rossi's terribly-titled *Unbearable Lightness*, then described it as a 'how-to manual'. Another referred to Marya Hornbacker's *Wasted*, something of a cult book within this community of illness, as 'triggering as fuck'. (I love this term, triggering, how it makes it sound like we're all packed tight with emotional gunpowder and coiled, ever ready to misfire.)

I resisted too because I've been frustrated by so many of the narratives of mental illness I've seen in the media, in film, in literature too, which can't seem to hold together the complexities of recovering, of making mistakes and slipping backwards, of forgetting and relearning and forgetting again, of compromise and conditionality, or even the incredibly slow, repetitive and exhaustingly mundane nature of the process of getting better. The fall into illness, the difficulty of the illness itself, the realisation that something is wrong: these things can be accounted for, if not always easily, but everything that happens after we realise that we are ill and seek out help can't be tied up so neatly.

But my resistance softened recently, in part because I discovered a collection of essays — called *Going Hungry* — by writers who were writers before they became ill, not writers who become so because they had been ill. Many of them I already admired as writers, before knowing that we had our hungers in common: the poet Louise Glück, the novelist Jennifer Egan. Many wrote of lingering symptoms, of fears that their hunger might reassert itself at any time, some wrote of becoming well enough, though far from well. The poet Priscilla Becker writes of 'sett[ing] into a kind of working anorexia, not careening towards death, but…[still] disciplined, self-contained'; she quotes a friend of hers as saying 'It doesn't sound like you've been cured of anorexia, just that you've raised the bar a little.'

I recognise myself in this, still disciplined, still frugal, still tightly controlling of my meals; I still don't like others to cook for me, am still frightened by a wide range of perfectly ordinary foods. But I also think that this is how the curing works – by raising the bar just a little, and then raising it again and again: I know that some of the things I do without thinking, now – like eating a sandwich, even if it's the same meat-free and salad-heavy sandwich every day – were unimaginable to me once, but are terribly banal to write about.

Many wrote of continuing to work too hard or to 'overschedule', of continuing to be self-contained and difficult to get to know, of continuing to defer pleasure, of addictive behaviour, still, years later. One has written a book about adults who continue to live, long-term, at 'sub-clinical' status, well enough to evade diagnosis and the ever-tightening kind of control that my hunger once had for me, but still far from healthy; the oldest participant in her study was ninety-two years old.

I'm terribly afraid of living like this, sub-clinically, long-term. I know that I still I have to fight hard for my own health, but also that sometimes I still don't want to. I miss the simplicity of illness sometimes. Because the more acute pain is in trying to get better – and it's a pain that's chronic too – and in stripping away the protection, the insulation, the certainty that my hunger gave me.

More importantly, what I realised, reading the stories in *Going Hungry*, is that I've been resisting, too, telling my own story, or rather, telling all of my own story. Because I didn't want to be one of *those women*, the story that I tell, and that I've told myself, for years, is about how my physical condition made me into one of them. How the caprices of my body changed me into one of those women, that is, but not how I may well have been one of their number for a long time beforehand. I still think that what happened to me was the almost-inevitable consequence of a run of incredibly bad luck: that my physical illness, and the biochemical changes that starvation wrought on my body and mind as I waited for a diagnosis, combined with my drivenness and anxiousness to lead me to my hunger. But I recognise now within these other stories that my hunger was within me already, maybe even always. I've resisted telling this other story, I think, because I don't want to hear it myself.

The very first time I lost weight I did it on purpose. I was fifteen, maybe sixteen; I was by no means large, but not lean either, and I was uncomfortable in my skin. I didn't possess the easy, unselfconscious grace of my friends – the ballsy, glamorous Nina, dark-skinned and beautiful, who even at this age was buying Dior make-up and French lingerie, and wearing it with converse sneakers and Mambo singlets; the devil-may-care Anna who draped herself in black, whose hair and limbs were long and straight and glossy, who always carried a bag of lollies in her school backpack and once called me greedy when I took an extra chocolate from the bag that she was sharing around. (A teacher once told Anna that she 'didn't look like a lollies person', and I asked, somewhat masochistically, if I did, and he responded, 'You do, yes.' It's strange that I remember this now.)

I adored both girls with that teenage intensity of friendship that's ferocious, almost obsessive, crush-like, and never matched again in later life. My friends seemed brilliant, carelessly eccentric, and completely certain of themselves and their own minds. I was awkward and over-eager, always trying to keep up; I wore double-D bras and brightly-coloured chenille shirts. I made tie-dyed pants in textiles class and pinned novelty buttons shaped like sunflowers and Volkswagons in my unruly hair. I know I wanted to dress differently and unusually, because I felt that I was different and unusual; perhaps all teenagers, to some extent feel this way. I cultivated brashness, a deliberately unfeminine brazenness that I never quite believed in, but that I still catch myself falling back into today. But these too, I know now, are common traits in the kinds of people who develop anorexia, complex and competing desires to stand out and to fit in, to be unique but be accepted, to push away the people who we don't think will quite accept us, yet to long for them to take us to their hearts.

When I was fifteen, maybe sixteen, I borrowed my mother's instructional pamphlets from the weight-loss program she attended every week in the hall of my old primary school; each food, and every ten minutes of exercise was accorded a number of points, to be credited and debited across the day. There was a booklet that listed an exhaustive set of foods by type and brand and flavour, a card with a movable wheel for calculating the value of anything not listed, according to its energy and fat content. I remember doing this, and yet I say, still, that I've never counted calories. I started walking of an afternoon, around the looping streets and bushland fire trails of my suburb, or caught a different bus that only stopped a good twenty-minute march away from home. I lost weight, and I liked it, and another friend referred to me as 'new and improved'. I remember packing my own lunchbox, minimally, and yet I say, still, that I never had restrictive tendencies until I became unwell.

In my second or third year of outpatient treatment, when I was twenty-six or twenty-seven, I was waiting in the corridor of the hospital clinic, with its pastel walls and its over-excited heating system always cranked right up to keep our under-insulated bodies warm, when a woman walked up to the counter from the doorway, her waist cinched in a wide elastic belt, black and ribby over her striped dress. I recognised her from my high school, she'd been a prefect in my year, one of those whip-smart and unshakable girls, always groomed and composed, stately behind the assembly lectern. I assumed she was at work – our school was an academically selective girls' school, we'd been told since we arrived there that we were the *crème de la crème*, the doctors, scientists, leaders of tomorrow – it made sense that she'd studied medicine and was there to confer with a colleague. When I greeted her she said she had come in to see someone, and I thought then that she meant a friend. She later told me she'd assumed the same of me, both of us unable to imagine that the other brilliant teenager we'd known had ended up as a patient within those walls.

When I told this story to my sister, who hadn't felt at home within our high school and had always held a healthy teenage disdain towards its rhetoric of guaranteed success and limitless achievement, she was nonplussed. 'I don't think that's a coincidence,' she said.

I've always said that I thrived in my high school, largely because it was a small community, and a place where intelligence was admired, and eccentricity supported. I easily became notorious as someone who had both in spades. The school was, by the senior years, hotly competitive: I've been thinking a lot lately about the girl who was my fiercest rival in English, the subject where we both sought to stake our claim, how she never ate at school but always maintained that she had a big afternoon tea when she got home, and how I dropped only three marks across the entire year's assessments but was devastated when I did so. (In her poem 'Dedication to Hunger', Louise Glück writes about her fifteen-year-old, anorexic self 'I felt/ what I feel now, aligning these words −/ it is the same need to be perfect/ of which death is the mere byproduct.') We had another friend, Nina's best friend, who for a time seemed to live off jellybeans and green apples.

In my senior years, my school allowed me to enrol in an extra unit of German, even though no other student wanted to do the course – I was allocated three lessons per week, one-on-one with a language teacher who already had a full teaching load, such was the school's faith in my abilities. I was disciplined, I worked hard, and my achievement was always tangible and immediate: we were ranked against our classmates every time we were assessed. Lisa Halliday writes about the drive for 'objective standards', for the measurement and assessment of her self, as being critical to the development of her disease; because I never used the bathroom scales to set these standards, like most others with my illness, I never realised that this too was part of me, even then.

When I was fifteen, I remember being set an assignment in the subject that I liked least of all, Personal Development and Health; we had to write a poem called 'About Me' (it must have been an exercise for self-esteem) and I stalled and avoided the task for months beyond its due date, until I was told that I would fail the subject unless I handed something in. I couldn't say, at the time, why I wouldn't do the task; one of the reasons I remember this so clearly is that I'd never not handed in work before. Louise Glück writes that in her school years, her anorexia served to 'construct, in the only possible way when the means [were] so limited, a plausible self;' she adds 'I had great resources of will and no self'. More and more now this makes sense to me, I was modelling myself off the friends around me (perhaps all teenagers are like this) but I always thought that they'd eventually spot my fraudulence and catch me out.

I wrote my first poems at school, as a major work for my final exams. I read these again recently, and was horrified to realise that one of the last poems in the sequence is about a teenage girl who isn't eating, who is over-exercising to the point of dizziness, who wants to be empty and glossy and untouchable. A girl who 'watches her stomach's juices/ turn to/ attack her own body' and who 'knows she's a martyr/ a hero/ a warrior/ and her will is stronger/ than theirs.' A girl who is obviously circumstantially similar to how I was then – she lives near an athletics oval, catches the train to school, refuses to shave her legs. I know the poem wasn't auto-biographical, that I was imagining myself into a character, the way all writers do, but it's the insight in the poem that chills me now – the anger in the girl's running, the distance she feels from others, the almost fetishistic listing of foods she won't allow herself, the way she feels the grease from what she does eat on her lips. I didn't know what lay ahead, but I seem to have been already writing myself into an anorectic body, preparing myself for an injury that I hadn't suffered yet and the scale of which I never could have foreseen.

I was seventeen when I wrote that poem. It was barely eighteen months later, that my physical illness developed.

In the interim, I started university, something I had been looking forward to with an almost itchy anticipation. I had been told that I would have the best years of my life there, that I'd flourish, but instead, I just felt lost. I was studying media, because I only knew that I liked writing and had high marks – too high, my school careers advisor had once said, to 'throw away' on a plain arts degree. It seemed like I was one of only about a dozen students in the hundred-strong cohort in my course who hadn't gone to a private school, learnt debating and a woodwind instrument, and paid their university fees upfront. They were mainly young women, and a kind and class of women I'd had no contact with before – just as they had had no contact with people like me. They asked each other where they'd gone to school, and placed each other accordingly and simply. They carried their notebooks and textbooks in those shiny cardboard bags with rope handles that designer clothes shops use, and wore, as I wrote at the time, 'sunglasses wider than their arses'. Perhaps the differences between us felt embodied, even then.

In the last hospital program I attended, another patient, a chatty, blonde-bobbed woman, spoke about her first year at university. She had been one of these private-school girls, but had chosen to study in a regional university, and had not known how to place herself within its student body because none of the students she spoke to cared where they or she had gone to school. Our experiences, I laughed, were inversions of each other, but it wasn't until months later that I realised that inversions are more similar than they are opposite.

When I started university, most of my friends from high school – those women whom I'd unconsciously shaped myself off for years – got swept up in their new lives and new friendships and fell suddenly and completely out of my orbit. I felt Nina's loss most keenly. I remember calling her on my brand-new and first-ever mobile phone one day when we were supposed to meet for lunch in Chinatown; she didn't answer and I rang again, and again, not yet knowing how uncool this was, too eager, too graceless again.

Where I did start to make friends was through a dazzling, chatty strawberry-blonde from my German class, a woman with the same brazen insouciance as Nina and the same casual ease in her slender body. Charlie's friends were mostly scholarship students, they were involved in theatre, in bands, in student politics and even national-level competitive Scrabble; they were witty and devastatingly ironic. When I talk about them now, I call them proto-hipsters; but at the time, I just felt gauche and painfully ordinary beside them, beneath them. At university, too, those objective standards that I'd previously met so well, those marks and rankings, fell away, and I couldn't figure out how to measure myself without them.

Sarah Haight, whose illness began in her first year of university, writes that she found herself, like me, like my blonde-bobbed fellow patient, no longer 'a local celebrity, or even one of the smartest girls in the class'. She writes that, when she found herself without the 'constant external affirmation' of achievement that she'd experienced, like me, at school, she was anchorless, bereft. It's so simple a step for hunger to come to inhabit this void, for denial to become a new kind of achievement, a shrinking body to clearly delineate a self that feels amorphous. Anorexia has rituals, rules and structure; I know that part of what confused me in my first year at university was the complete absence of these things.

I know too that I dieted in that first year, because I had been diagnosed with polycystic ovarian syndrome, a relatively benign endocrine disorder that something like a quarter of all women have; the doctor had warned me that the condition can increase the risk of diabetes and so it was important to avoid becoming overweight. I had gained some weight that year, going out for lunch with classmates during long breaks between lectures in the nearby café-cultured suburbs so unlike where I'd grown up, and having late-afternoon drinks on the balcony of the university bar (I drank lurid-coloured pre-mix then). They called this 'fresher spread' at the university I attended, the phenomenon common enough to earn a colloquial name. I remember eagerly mentioning my diet to Charlie at a Thai restaurant one night, thinking somehow it would earn me some kind of praise; instead she crinkled up her nose and turned away. (Charlie also asked me, the next year, after my physical condition had developed, why I was eating my lunch at all given that it was making me throw up.)

In the story that I tell, and that I've told myself for years, this diet – barely a year before I first fell ill – never features. I had almost forgotten that it happened at all. Because what happened next – the months of unexplained and unconscious vomiting, the rounds of frustrating and often condescending consultations with doctors and gastroenterologists, the rapid weight loss that soon left me and those around me terrified – all of this is so much more dramatic and easily narrated, as well as so much more unusual, that the diet seemed unimportant in comparison.

So too this: in the year that I first become ill, when I ran into women who I'd been to school with, they never failed to tell me that I looked wonderful, that I looked different. When I went out for meals in groups I now had to be catered for, given special menus or different dishes, I was no longer just another part of the crowd. When I was hungry, I felt alert and intense and alive along every inch of my skin, and I felt unassailable in a way that I hadn't felt for years. Jennifer Egan writes 'I felt as if I were finally coming into focus, hard and sharp and light, released from the bulky packaging of my sadness.' Louise Glück writes of sacrificing her 'interfering flesh' until her 'limbs were free/ of blossom and subterfuge', I shared this sense of paring back to something that feels bare and bold and true.

My illness, that is, began to give me the structure that I felt anchorless without, came to give me the distinction that I couldn't find anymore in the huge and ever-mobile population of university. It felt definite when I was anything but. And pushing through hunger, past the physical weakness and tiredness that it imposes on the body was a new kind of achievement, and one that no one else around me came close to being able to attain. My illness made me different from the people I already felt alien to. They needed, I didn't, and I didn't feel anything as keenly any more, my body and mind both numbed by malnutrition. I had found a way to possess myself, my own kind of grace.

This too, I know, is only a part of the whole story. My illness, and the long months that it took to find a diagnosis, affected my cognition and emotions and behaviour just as prolonged hunger affected those young men in Minnesota. I know that my fear of throwing up couldn't help but make me nervous around food. (I've experienced this again recently, watching my boyfriend react to my unexpected bouts of vomiting, listening on as he tries to find a reason or a pattern or a way to prevent it from happening next time; anyone, I realised, would become wary of food in my position.) I know now that many people first experience disordered eating as a result of physical illness; and that the intense pitch of my emotions makes me vulnerable to mental illness. All of these things are still true; it's just that I recognise I've always been more comfortable with these parts of the narrative, no doubt because – like all anorexics, ironically enough – I can't stand the idea of being common, of being a cliché, even and especially in my illness.

I don't know, though, where acknowledging all of this leaves me. I maintained, for years that it didn't matter exactly how my disorder developed or took control, simply that it did, and the important thing was learning how I was going to pull myself clear. I wonder now if these elisions in the narrative have kept their dark power, somehow, for remaining in the shadows of the story that I've told myself in the meantime. I know that my hunger, my illness allowed me to fashion a new self. I have been struggling now for several years, to find a way to be without my hunger, and that in the process, I so often feel gauche and graceless, uncomfortably thin-skinned, just like all those years before. (I often joke that recovering is like a second adolescence, made all the more acute by the reignition of my hormones — I've lived for so long without both ragged lust and raging mood swings that they always catch me by surprise.)

On a recent weekend, I found myself walking through the grounds of my old university — I now live just streets away, and was crossing through it as a scenic shortcut to a bus stop I needed to use. I walked past the residential colleges, past the bar used by the arts students, the grandiose main sandstone building where my first media lectures had been held. The carillon bells were playing, so I stopped in the shadow of the building, on the clipped, plush lawns, to listen, and was overtaken, suddenly, by a swift, deep sadness of place. For the girl that I was, I suppose, lost and desperate and confused within those walls, and so terribly alone. For the girl who had this hunger already within her, and for the woman who I've been, who I've become. The bells stopped and I stood back up. I brushed the dirt from my jeans and kept walking.

A Note on Sources

A number of works have been important to this book – and to my own understanding of my experiences and illness:

In Colombo

This chapter draws on ideas discussed in *As A Weasel Sucks Eggs: An Essay on Melancholy and Cannibalism* by Daniel Birnbaum and Anders Olsson (Sternberg Press, 2008) and Maud Ellman's *The Hunger Artists: Starving, Writing and Imprisonment* (Harvard UP, 1993). For more information on Sri Lanka's civil war, see William McGowan's *Only Man is Vile: The Tragedy of Sri Lanka* (Picador, 1992).

In Berlin

This chapter draws on Sharman Apt Russell's *Hunger: An Unnatural History* (Basic Books, 2009) for information about Ancel Key's Minnesota Experiment; and on Leonard Tushnet's *The Uses of Adversity: Studies of Starvation in the Warsaw Ghetto* (AS Barnes and Co, 1966).

In Miniature

This chapter quotes directly from the following sources: Melinda Alliker Rabb's 'Johnson, Lilliput and Eighteenth-Century Miniature', *Eighteenth-Century Studies* 46:2 (2013), Gaston Bachelard's *The Poetics of Space* (Beacon Press 1964), Steven Millhauser's 'The Fascination of the Miniature', *Grand*

Street 2:4 (1983), and Susan Stewart's *On Longing: Narratives of the Miniature, the Gigantic, the Souvenir, the Collection* (John Hopkins UP, 1984). The poem 'What She Could Not Tell Him' is by Denise Levertov, and published in her collection *Breathing the Water* (New Directions, 1987).

In Increments

Information about the history of treatments for 'hysterical anorexia' draws on Joan Jacobs Brumberg's seminal book *Fasting Girls: The History of Anorexia Nervosa* (Plume, 1989).

Information about the anorectic brain's responses to eating comes from Laura Hill's talk 'Eating Disorders from the Insider Out' accessible at http://bit.ly/1GaA32Y. The American studies referred to are being undertaken at the University of California, by a team lead by Walter Kaye. Two of Kaye's papers resulting from this work are 'Brain imaging studies reveal neurobiology of eating disorders' in *ScienceDaily*, 10 April 2013, and 'Hunger does not Motivate Reward in Women Remitted from Anorexia Nervosa' in *Biological Psychiatry* 77:7.

In Books I

The book discussed in this chapter is *For Love Alone* by Christina Stead (Imprint, 1991). *For Love Alone* was first published in the UK in 1945, and in Australia in 1966.

In Books II

The collections of poetry referred to at the beginning of this chapter are *The Darwin Poems* by Emily Ballou (UWA Press, 2009) and *The Bee Hut* by Dorothy Porter (Black Inc, 2009). Also discussed here are Tim Winton's *Cloudstreet* (Penguin, 1991) and Carmel Bird's *The Bluebird Café* (Vintage, 1990).

In Group

This chapter discusses John Berryman's *Recovery/Delusions* (Dell, 1974); and quotes directly from his poetry collection *77 Dream Songs* (Farrar, Straus and Giroux, 1964). The quote from Wallace Stevens comes from his book *The Necessary Angel: Essays on Reality and the Imagination* (Alfred A Knopf, 1951).

In Hindsight

This chapter discusses the book *Going Hungry* edited by Kate Taylor (Anchor, 2008). Thank you to Ceridwen Dovey for introducing me to this work. Quotes from Louise Glück's poem 'Dedication to Hunger' are taken from her *Poems 1962–2012* (Farrar, Straus and Giroux, 2012).

The epigram for this book is taken from Gwen Harwood's poem 'Past and Present', published in her *Collected Poems 1943–1995* (UQP, 2003), edited by Allison Hoddinot and Gregory Kratzmann.

Acknowledgements

The people who have been important to this book, and to me, along the way are so many and their contributions so important that they're difficult to acknowledge, without also admitting that this list is written in the spirit of a healthy imperfection and in full knowledge that the gesture is a small one only. Thank you firstly to my family, whose love, patience and kindness have been enduring – and undoubtedly an endurance at times. And to my urban family: especially Susan Wijngaarden, Tim Curry, Tim Peters, and also Nicola Vartuli, Ava Schacherl-Lam, Elle Warren, Elena Gomez, Sara Jones, Jayna Staykov, Alex Scott and Pippa Jaminon. Thank you to Patrick O'Rourke. Thank you to Elizabeth Hall.

Writing-wise, my thanks to Sam Twyford-Moore, Rebecca Giggs, Sam Cooney, Kate Middleton, Pip Smith, Angela Meyer, Jen Craig and Eileen Chong for conversation, commiseration and ideas; as well as the fabulous folks at Sweatshop: especially Mohammed Ahmed, Luke Carman, Peter Polites, Felicity Castagna, Lachlan Brown, Tamar Chnorhokian, Arda Barut, Rebecca Landon, George Toseski, Peta Murphy and Amanda Yeo; thank you to Alice Grundy and David Henley; and to Ivor Indyk and Evelyn Juers for unending support and encouragement.

Some of the essays in this book have previously appeared in *Sydney Review of Books*, *Seizure*, *The Lifted Brow* and *Overland*; or have been performed as part of Sweatshop showcases. Thank you to the editors involved.

Finally, to all of the men and women I've encountered on the way, fighting the good fight: you know who you are, how wonderful you are, and how important you have been. Thank you, and of course, luck and courage to you always.

Fiona Wright's poetry book *Knuckled* (published by Giramondo in 2011) won the Dame Mary Gilmore Award for a first collection. Her poems and essays have been published in the *Australian, Meanjin, Island, Overland, The Lifted Brow, Seizure* and *HEAT*.